Marriage Bonds
and
Ministers' Returns
of
Southampton County
Virginia
- 1750-1810 -

I0094170

Compiled By:
Catherine Lindsay Knorr

Southern Historical Press, Inc.
Greenville, South Carolina

SOUTHERN HISTORICAL PRESS, INC.
PO BOX 1267
Greenville, SC   29601

ISBN #0-89308-255-4

Printed in the United States of America

In Memory of

MARY HALL POLLARD

(Mrs. James Claiborne Pollard)

who, as librarian and archivist

in the Virginia State Library,

helped countless thousands search

the records; who daily gave gen-

erously of her time and vast know-

ledge of Virginiana to further the

efforts of those searchers.

Died 13 September 1953

WORROSQUYOAKE
ORIGINAL SHIRE
1634-1637

|

ISLE OF WIGHT
1637

|

SOUTHAMPTON
1749

A HORNBOOK OF VIRGINIA HISTORY
CHART 7, PAGE 23

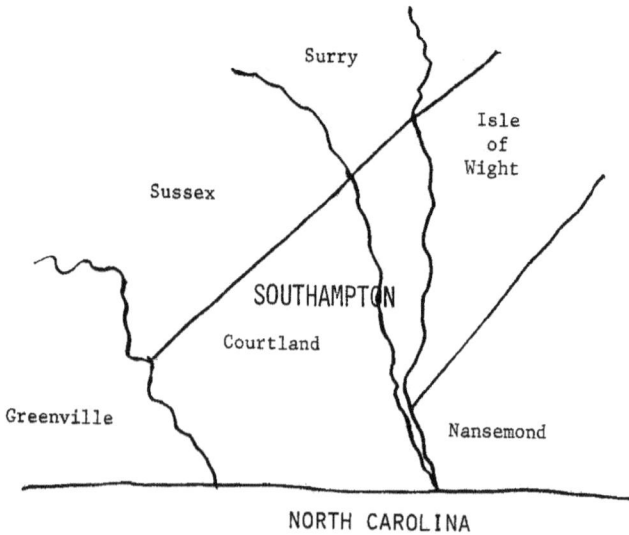

Surry

Isle
of
Wight

Sussex

SOUTHAMPTON

Courtland

Greenville

Nansemond

NORTH CAROLINA

PUBLISHER'S PREFACE

Mrs. Knorr died in 1975, and after her death these books of marriage records were kept in print and sold by her late husband. Upon his death, they became the property of her grandson, Hal Wyche Greer, III, of Marietta, Georgia, who continued to sell them on a limited basis.

In mid-1981 I sought to find Mr. Greer to discuss with him the possibility of obtaining the exclusive publishing and sales rights to these 14 titles. In due time, Mr Greer and I were able to negotiate a contract for my exclusive sales and publication rights to these books. It was agreed that Mr. Greer would have a final voice on the changing of the format of any of these titles when they needed to be reprinted. I suggested to Mr. Greer that when these various books sold out and a reprinting had to be done, that for the sake of cost, I would publish them in a 6" x 9" page size, but that the format and style would remain the same, and this was agreed upon.

The reader is cautioned to note that these new 6 x 9 pages are typed verbatim from Mrs. Knorr's original copy, and page by page, so that new indexing was not required. It was also decided that when a book went out of print, it would be retyped on an electric typewriter with a carbon ribbon for better legibility. As publisher, I felt it was important to call to the attention of the reader these changes and the reason for eventually bringing out all of these titles in a 6 x 9 book.

The Rev. S. Emmett Lucas, Jr.
Publisher

PREFACE

Southampton County was authorized by an Act passed in 1748 but the actual dividing of Isle of Wight County did not take place until a year later. The second Act was passed by the General Assembly on 30 April 1749.

Order Book No. I states that the first court was held at the home of Elizabeth Ricks on 8 June 1749. The first clerk of Southampton County was Richard Kello. Benjamin Ruffin was the first sheriff. John Person and Joseph Gray took the oaths of Justice of the Peace and Judge in Chancery, administered to them by Jesse Brown and Benjamin Simmons. Nathaniel Ridley, Thomas Jarrell, Etheldred Taylor, Howell Edmonds, Jesse Brown, Benjamin Simmons, Albridgton Jones, James Ridley, Peter Butts, Samuel Blow and Thomas Williamson, constituted Gentlemen Justices.

The Court appointed Benjamin Branch, Arthur Arrington, Joseph Cobb, Samuel Kindred and John Brown as constables.

The new county is one of 13 that Virginia names in honor of prominent Englishmen (Long p. 63). Sir Henry Wriothesley, Earl of Southampton (Robinson p. 191). Sir Henry Wriothesley was the only patron William Shakespeare ever acknowledged. To him he dedicated "Venus and Adonis" and "The Rape of Lucrece."

The Earl of Southampton, born 6 October 1573; died 10 November 1624, was made a Knight of the Garter 1603 (Shaw's "Knights of England" I, 30). He was called Lord Wriothesley until created Earl of Southampton 21 July 1603. He was Councillor of the Virginia Company 23 May 1609; Treasurer and later Governor until his death in 1624. (Complete Peerage 2nd Ed. Vol. XII, pp. 128-131.)

The county seat of Southampton is Courtland, as pleasant a village as ever was. The priceless records are presided over by Miss Besse Thomas Shands who is the soul of courtesy, and help-fulness.

My first visit to Courtland was with Mrs. Lewis L Chapman of Smithfield, Virginia. She was abstracting the wills while I was madly copying the marriages. We had the happiest time working from "kin to can't" as our colored people say...

...Some names are, inevitably, used interchangeably as Kirby - Kerby, Kinchen - Kitchen, Joyner - Joiner, Wilson - Willson, Wester - Westray, Garner - Gardner and Luter and Suter are almost impossible to distinguish one from the other.

Mr. J. W. Dudley of the Virginia Archives, Richmond, has kindly checked all discrpanceis for me.

This second edition of the Southampton Marriages corrects all the omissions and errors in the first edition (1948) and adds ten years to the scope of the work. I hope you like it.

Catherine Lindsay Knorr

P. S. Acrill Lamb out of place, excuse it, please.

MARRIAGES OF SOUTHAMPTON COUNTY, VIRGINIA

1750 - 1810

27 August 1801. ARTHUR ADAMS and ELIZABETH REESE, dau. of Sally Reese. Sur. Adam Ivey. Wit. John Reese and Samuel Kello. p. 145

1 January 1784. BENJAMIN ADAMS and CELIA REESE. Minister's returns p. 634

15 May 1797. EDWIN ADAMS and JANE RIDLEY. Sur. William Blunt. Wit. John D. Haussmann and William Wright. p. 114

16 February 1778. HENRY ADAMS and MARY GARRITY both of Nottoway Parish. Sur. John Adams. Wit. Samuel Kello. p. 25

15 July 1799. JOHN ADAMS and SARAH MINNIS. Sur. Burwell Rollings. Wit. Samuel Kello, Jr. Married 18 July by Rev. Drewry Lane. p. 127

27 May 1800. MATTHEW ADAMS and SALLY WINDHAM. Sur. John Clark. Wit. Samuel Kello. p. 135

10 February 1791. MOSES ADAMS and TAMOR ADAMS, son of Thomas Adams. Sur. Peterson Ivey. Wit. John D. Haussmann. p. 70

10 March 1809. ROBERT ADAMS and NANCY ELY, consent of Burwell Branch. Sur. Francis Branch. Wit. Samuel Kello. p. 190

19 July 1789. BENJAMIN ALLEN and MARY BRITT. Sur. James Allen. Wit. Samuell Kello. Married 22 June by Rev. D.C. Barrow. p. 60

8 January 1789. RICHARD ALLEN and PRISCILLA LAWRENCE. Sur. Jacob Lawrence. p. 57

13 March 1783. JAMES ALSOBROOK and TEMPCE (Temperance) WOMACK. Minister's returns p. 632

13 January 1763. WILLIAM ANDERSON of Surry Co. and ELIZABETH CHAPPELL, dau. of Thomas Chappell who is surety. Wit. Richard Kello. p. 8

17 November 1800. AMBROSE ANDREWS and SALLY WESTBROOKE. Sur. Will P. Westbrooke. p. 139

4 November 1798. BARTLEY ANDREWS and SILVIA WILLIAMSON, dau. of Absalom Williamson. Sur. Joseph Williamson. Wit. David Williamson and Samuel Kello. p. 123

17 November 1789. BENJAMIN ANDREWS and OLIVE WASHINGTON. Sur. Elias Herring. p. 63

1 February 1794. DAVID ANTHONY ANDREWS and MARY COKER. Sur. Thomas Philips. Wit. John D. Haussmann. p. 95

1

2 December 1801. HENRY ANDREWS and REBECCA BOOTH. Sur. Samuel Kello, Jr. Married 19 December by Rev. Burwell Barrett. p. 147

29 November 1787. JAMES ANDREWS and PATSY HERRING. Sur. Elias Herring. Wit. Samuel Kello. Married by Rev. D.C. Barrow. p. 53

30 April 1781. JOHN ANDREWS and LUCY BUTTS. Sur. William Whitfield. Wit. Richard Kello. p. 30

24 September 1796. JOHN ANDREWS and ELIZABETH BOOTH. Sur. James _____. Wit. Samuel Kello. p. 109

21 June 1800. RICHARD ANDREWS and PEGGY STEPHENSON. Sur. Samuel Kello. Wit. John Stephenson. p. 236

12 March 1792. ROBERT ANDREWS and RHODA DREWRY. Sur. Joseph Vick. Wit. John D. Haussmann. p. 80

8 April 1773. WILLIAM ANDREWS and ANNE PITMAN, dau. of John and Elizabeth Pitman who consent. Sur. Richard Blow of St. Luke's Parish. Wit. Richard Kello, Luke Browning and Giles Cook. p. 19

9 October 1783. HARDY APPLEWHAITE and CHARLOTTE CLIFTON, dau. of Sarah Clifton. Sur. William Clifton. p. 37

17 May 1756. HENRY APPLEWHAITE and ANN HARRIS. Sur. Benjamin Lewis. Wit. Richard Kello and Thomas Blunt. p. 3

14 October 1784. JOHN APPLEWHITE and REBECCA MOORE. Sur. John Simmons. p. 38

26 January 1792. LUKE ARCHER and HONOUR ARTIS, dau. of Lewis Artis. Sur. Newit Vick. Married 27 Jan. by Rev. Benjamin Barnes. p. 78

17 February 1800. HENRY ARRINGTON and MARTHA KIRBY. Sur. Samuel Drewry. Wit. Samuel Kello, Jr. and Lucy Drewry. Note: Samuel Drewry married Lucy Arrington 7 November 1798. p. 133

10 November 1790. JOHN ARRINGTON and ELIZABETH MOORE. Sur. Thomas Pond. Wit. Samuel Kello. p. 68

12 December 1796. JOHN ARRINGTON and JULIA KIRBY, consent of John Kirby, parent or guardian of Julia. Sur. Joseph Laine. Wit. John D. Haussmann. p. 111

16 November 1758. WILLIAM ARRINGTON and SABRA WILLIAMS, dau. of Chaplin Williams, Jr. Sur. Benjamin Davis. Wit. Bryde Williams, Charles Carter and Richard Kello. p. 5

21 August 1783. BURWELL ARTIS and ANGEY HURST. Ministers' returns p. 633

30 December 1801. CHARLES ARTIS (or Artist) and MASON POWELL. Sur. Evans Pope. Wit. Samuel Kello. p. 148

23 February 1796. EDMUND ARTIS and NANNY EVANS. Sur. Jordin Artis. Wit. Samuel Kello. p. 106

10 September 1800. JOHN ARTIS and PHEREBE CATON. Sur. Nathan Worrell. Wit. Samuel Kello, Jr. p. 138

15 February 1802. JOHN ARTIS (Artist) and BLYTHA POWELL. Sur. John Pope. Wit. Evans Pope. p. 149

30 December 1801. RICHARD ARTIS (or Artist) and REBECCA BANKS. Sur. Evans Pope. Wit. Asa Beal. p. 148

13 September 1760. JEPTHA (Jephtha) ATHERTON and SARAH TYNES. Sur. Richard Kello. Wit. Jona. Godwin. p. 6

11 March 1763. JEPTHAH ATHERTON and ELIZABETH JARRETT (widow) of St. Luke's Parish. Sur. Peter Butts of Nottoway Parish. p. 8

25 September 1781. HARDY ATK____ and ____ ____. Ministers' returns p. 630

7 November 1787. JOHN ATKINS and OLIVE HART. Sur. Joseph Hart. Wit. Samuel Kello. p. 53

29 December 1789. ELIAS ATKINSON and JENNETT EDMUNDS. Sur. Thomas Porter. Wit. Samuel Kello. p. 64

30 December 1791. ELIAS ATKINSON and JENNETT EDWARDS. Sur. Jonas Edmunds. Wit. John D. Haussmann. Married by Rev. Robert Murrell who says Jenet Edmunds. p. 77

1 January 1803. HOWELL ATKINSON and SALLY BURGES. Sur. John Gray. Wit. Samuel Kello. p. 152

22 April 1784. JAMES ATKINSON, JR. and MIRIAM JOHNSTON. Ministers' returns p. 634

25 October 1785. JAMES ATKINSON, JR. and ELIZABETH CHANNELL. Ministers' returns p. 636

6 March 1783. JESSE ATKINSON and PAMELIA SPEED. Ministers' returns p. 632

19 June 1774. JOHN ATKINSON and MARY JELKS. Sur. William Jelks. Wit. Richard Kello. p. 21

7 October 1797. JOSEPH ATKINSON and PRISCILLA EDWARDS, dau. of Micajah Edwards who consents and is surety. Wit. Samuel Kello and B. Drew. p. 115

3 December 1791. SAMUEL ATKINSON and LUCY HART. Sur. Thomas Hart. Wit. John D. Haussmann. p. 76

24 February 1786. THOMAS AUBERRY and MARY HART. Ministers' returns p. 636

23 December 1806. JOHN AVENT and SUCKEY THORPE. Sur. F. Clements. Wit. Samuel Kello. p. 175

6 June 1780. ABSALOM BAILEY and HOLLAND BOOTH. Sur. Richard Kello. Wit. Samuel Mesam. p. 29

13 July 1784. DEMPSEY BAILEY and SALLY EDWARDS. Ministers' returns p. 634

16 March 1792. EDWARD BAILEY and SARAH SCOTT. Sur. Edmund Cosby. Wit. John D. Haussmann. p. 81

21 September 1809. GEORGE BAILEY and ELIZABETH CLAYTON HOLMES, dau. of Solomon Holmes. Sur. Edwin Delk. Wit. Harrison Minton. p. 194

22 August 1778. JACOB BAILEY and AMY CRENSHAW of St. Luke's Parish, dau. of Thomas Crenshaw. Sur. William Kitching. Wit. Samuel Kello and John Crenshaw. p. 26

27 November 1797. MATTHEW BAILEY and SUSANNA LANE, dau. of Drewry Lane. Sur. William Summerell. Wit. Samuel Kello, Jr. Married 28 Nov. by Rev. John Ellis. p. 117

28 December 1793. PHILIP BAILEY and ELIZABETH MEGLAMRE, dau. of John Meglamre. Sur. Wyatt Bailey. p. 93

20 January 1800. SAMUEL BAILEY and MARTHA DELOACH. Sur. Charles Bailey. Wit. Samuel Kello. Married 23 Jan. by Rev. William Hargrave. p. 132

27 January 1783. WALTER BAILEY and SARAH DAVIS, dau. of Sarah Mitchell. Sur. Archer Davis. Wit. Samuel Kello. p. 35

4 May 1776. WILLIAM BAILEY and SARAH JENKINGS. Sur. John Bailey. Wit. Samuel Kello. p. 23

9 October 1801. WILLIAM BAILEY and BETSEY BRIGGS. Married by
Rev. William Hargrave. Ministers' returns p. 651

17 December 1803. WILLIAM BAILEY and ALSEY BRYANT. Sur. Bailey
Bryant. Wit. Bolton Pierce. See William Railey. p. 157

27 November 1804. LITTLEBERRY BAMES and NANCY EDWARDS. Sur.
Thomas Velvin. Wit. William Turner. Married by Rev. Benjamin
Barnes, Methodist. p. 163

23 May 1786. WALTER BALLARD and BECKEY TAYLOR. Sur. Sampson
Pitman. Wit. Francis Young, Jr., E.R. Kello and Lucy Taylor.
E.R. Kello was Elizabeth Ridley Kello who married William Kello
23 Aug. 1778 as Elizabeth Ridley Taylor. Beckey probably her
daughter. Married 25 May by Rev. George Gurley, Rector St.
Luke's Parish, Episcopal Church. p. 46

27 February 1798. DAVID BALLENTINE and POLLY JOHNSON. Sur.
Benjamin Johnson. Wit. Samuel Kello, Jr. p. 119

9 January 1794. BRITAIN BARNES and RACHEL POPE. Sur. William
Pope. Wit. John D. Haussmann. p. 93

31 May 1789. JOHN BANKS and MILDRED VALENTINE. Both of
Scurry county. Married by Rev. D.C. Barrow. Ministers' returns
642

11 November 1767. WILLIAM BANNER (Bonner) and SYLVIA TYUS.
Sur. Charles Cosby. Wit. Edward Fisher. p. 12

16 March 1807. HENRY BANTA and CHARITY GREEN. Sur. Jordan
Jackson. Wit. Benjamin Cobb. This name may be Banton. p. 177

27 October 1803. LEWIS BARDEN and SARAH TANN, about 25 years
old. Sur. Matt Williams. Wit. Thomas Lain, Samuel Kello.
Married 28 Oct. by Rev. Drewry Lane. p. 156

19 August 1786. BENJAMIN BARHAM and SARAH NICOLSON. Sur.
Jesse Cooper. Wit. Samuel Kello. Married 24 Aug. by Rev. John
Meglamre, Baptist. p. 47

1 October 1790. BENJAMIN BARHAM and HANNAH BITTLE. Married
by Rev. Robert Murrell. Ministers' returns p. 646

12 May 1791. BENJAMIN BARHAM and ELIZABETH SMITH. Sur.
Edward Fisher. Wit. John D. Haussmann. Married by Rev. John
Meglamre, Baptist. p. 73

11 June 1795. BENJAMIN TAYLOR BARHAM and MABEL DUPREY (Dupree).
Sur. John Barlow, Jr. Wit. John D. Haussmann. p. 102

25 February 1772. CHARLES BARHAM and ANN ARRINGTON (widow).
Sur. James Barnham. Wit. Richard Kello. p. 18

8 November 1774. JOHN BARHAM and MARY APPLEWHAITE. Sur.
Henry Applewhaite. Wit. Samuel Kello. p. 21

11 June 1778. JOHN BARHAM and NANCY MOORE. Sur. William
McEldoe (McAldoe). Wit. Samuel Kello. p. 26

19 December 1808. JOHN BARHAM and REBECCA CLEMENTS. Sur.
Samuel Blunt. Wit. Benjamin Cobb and James Harrison. p. 187

18 December 1797. SAMUEL BARHAM and ELIZABETH FORT. Sur.
Benjamin Hines. Wit. Samuel Kello, Jr. p. 117

12 November 1772. WILLIAM BARHAM and SARAH THOMAS, dau. of
Henry Thomas, deceased; consent of Martha Thomas. Sur. John
Thomas Blow. Wit. Richard Kello and Thomas Judkins. p. 18

11 November 1790. EDMUND BARKER and REBECCA DAVIS. Sur.
Jesse Bryant. Wit. Samuel Kello. p. 68

17 September 1804. RIVER BARKER and POLLY HALLAMAN, dau. of
Rebecca Hallaman. Sur. John Barham. Wit. Benjamin Cobb.
Married 21 Sept. by Rev. Robert Murrell. p. 162

4 May 1798. JOHN BARLOW and SUSAN PARKER, both of St. Luke's
Parish. Sur. William Myrick. Wit. W. Evans. p. 120

30 July 1804. BENJAMIN BARNER and CHARLOTTE WASDON. Married
by Rev. Robert Murrell. See Benjamin Barner. Ministers'
returns p. 653

30 June 1804. BENJAMIN BARNER and CHARLOTTE WARDEN. Sur.
John Frances. See Benjamin Barmer. p. 161

8 December 1791. BAILY BARNES and MARY BARHAM. Sur. Edmund
Fisher. Wit. John D. Haussmann. Face of bond 1791 - back of
bond 1792. p. 76

25 September 1805. BENJAMIN BARNES and PEGGY DRAKE, dau. of
John Drake. Benjamin son of Jacob Barnes. Sur. William
Washington. Wit. Bolton Pierce. p. 167

31 July 1809. BOLLING BARNES and ELIZABETH NEWSUM. Sur.
James Rochelle. Married 3 Aug. by Rev. Benjamin Barnes,
Methodist. p. 193

15 April 1782. BUXTON BARNES and PARTHENIA POWELL, dau. of
John Powell. Sur. Kinchen Martin. Wit. Richard Kello,
William Andrews and Joseph Powell. p. 32

2 November 1793. CORDALL BARNES and PRISCILLA KENNEBREU. Jesse Cooper guardian of Priscilla. Sur. David Pope. Wit. John D. Haussmann. p. 91

20 August 1810. EDWIN BARNES and JULIA EDMUNDS, dau. of Jonas Edmunds. Sur. Willie Underwood. p. 201

20 November 1782. JACOB BARNES and MILLE DOYEL. Sur. Hardy Doyel. Wit. Samuel Kello. p. 34

11 September 1794. JACOB BARNES and WINIFRED WALLER. Sur. Eley Eli (at top of bond Ele Eley at bottom of bond.) Wit. John D. Haussmann. p. 98

19 November 1804. JACOB BARNES and LUCY BARRETT, dau. of Benjamin and Katharine Barrett. Sur. Thomas Barnes. Wit. Samuel Kello. Married 22 Nov. by Rev. Benjamin Barnes, Methodist. p. 162

10 February 1763. JAMES BARNES and ELIZABETH MYRICH, dau. of John Myrich. Sur. James Bell of Sussex Co. Wit. Richard Kello. p. 8

8 August 1771. JAMES BARNES of Sussex Co., and ELIZABETH JONES, dau. of James Jones who is security. No witness given. p. 17

5 December 1789. JOHN BARNES and CHERRY HOWELL. Married by Rev. George Gurley, Rector of St. Luke's Parish, Episcopal Church. Ministers' returns p. 645

6 April 1788. JOSEPH BARNES and SALLY DARDEN. Married by Rev. D.C. Barrow. Ministers' returns p. 640

18 June 1798. JOSIAH BARNES and LEVINIA BRITT, underage, consent of Arthur Whitehead and Sally Whitehead as to Levinia. Sur. Reuben Whitfield. Wit. Samuel Kello, Jr. and Elizabeth Nelms. p. 121

13 May 1784. MYRICK BARNES and NANCY JONES. Sur. John Myrick. Wit. Samuel Kello, William Newsom and Joseph Prince. Consent of William Myrick. p. 38

8 December 1785. MYRICK BARNES and PHEBE THORPE. Sur. Moses McKenny (McKinney). Wit. Francis Young, Jr. p. 42

10 January 1793. RANDALL BARNES and SELIA (Celia?) BLOW, dau. of John Blow. Sur. Burwell Beale. Wit. Samuel Kello. Written Randolph two places and Randall two places. p. 87

16 March 1807. THOMAS BARNES and DOROTHY DRAKE. Sur. Exum Vick. Wit. Benjamin Cobb. p. 178

1 April 1780. WILLIAM BARNES and MILLE WILLIAMS. Sur. William
Williams. p. 28

13 July 1785. WILLIAM BARNES and REBECCA FORT, consent of Selah
Fort. Wit. Samuel Kello. Consent only. Ministers' returns
21 July 1785. p. 41

20 January 1785. BENJAMIN BARRETT and CATHERINE BARNES.
Ministers' returns p. 635

15 February 1781. EDMUND BARRETT and MILLEY WORRELL of St.
Luke's Parish. Sur. Simon Barrett. Wit. Richard Kello. p. 29

3 February 1806. JAMES BARRETT and SALLY BRYANT, dau. of William
Bryant. Consent of Benjamin Turner for James Barrett. Sur.
Jacob Barnes. Wit. Bolton Pierce. Married 13 Feb. by Rev.
Exum Everett. p. 169

11 March 1809. JAMES BARRETT and NANCY G. TURNER. Sur. Jiles
Barrett. Wit. James Rochelle. Married 21 Mar. by Rev.
Benjamin Barnes, Methodist. p. 190

26 April 1809. JILES BARRETT and POLLY BYNUM, age 21. Sur.
Bennett Barnes. Wit. James Rochelle and Samuel Kello. Married
27 Apr. by Rev. Benjamin Barnes, Methodist. p. 191

20 May 1799. JORDAN BARRETT and ELIZABETH ENGLISH, dau. of
Nathan English. Sur. Dinon (Dixon) Forgason. Married 23
May by Rev. Benjamin Barnes, Methodist. p. 127

16 February 1784. NATHAN BARRETT and SALLY BARRETT. Ministers'
returns p. 634

5 September 1809. REUBIN BARRETT and ELIZABETH CLAY. Sur.
William Nash. Wit. John Rawls and Harrison Minton. Married
15 Sept. by Rev. Benjamin Barnes, Methodist. p. 194

16 September 1794. WILLIAM BARRETT and ELIZABETH BOWDEN
(Bowdoin). Sur. William Macky. Wit. John D. Haussmann. p. 98

19 November 1798. HENRY BARROW and ELIZABETH TURNER. Sur.
John Myrick. p. 123

20 March 1809. JOHN BARROW and MASON VICK. Sur. Charles
Bryant. Wit. James Rochelle and Jordan Johnson. Married
30 Mar. by Rev. Benjamin Barnes, Methodist. p. 190

12 March 1798. NATHAN BARROW and JUDITH CLARK, dau. of Rebecca
Clark. Sur. Elijah Johnson. Wit. Rebecca Johnson and William
Clark and Samuel Kello, Jr. p. 120

7 March 1786. SAMUEL BASDEN and MARTHA JOHNSON. Sur. Britain Johnson. Married by Rev. David Barrow. p. 45

5 March 1803. BURGESS BASS and ELIZABETH BARKER. Sur. Thomas Witteford. Wit. Benjamin Cobb. Married 17 Mar. by Rev. Robert Murrell. p. 153

16 July 1798. DREWRY BASS and POLLY THORPE. Sur. David Thomas. Wit. Samuel Kello, Jr. Polley Thorp in Ministers' returns 9 Aug. 1798. Married by Rev. Robert Murrell. p. 122

31 July 1793. EDWIN BASS and REBECCA REESE. Olive Reese guardian of Rebecca. Sur. Isham Thorpe. Wit. John D. Haussmann and Benjamin Williamson. p. 90

24 January 1804. HENRY BASS and LUCY SMITH. Married by Rev. Robert Murrell. Ministers' returns p. 652

11 April 1803. HOWELL BASS and CHARLOTTE NORVILE (Norvell), dau. of Mary Norvile. Sur. Rever Barker. Wit. Samuel Kello. Married by Rev. Robert Murrell. p. 154

27 March 1788. THOMAS BASS and SARAH ENGLISH, both of Isle of Wright County. Married by Rev. D.C. Barrow. Ministers' returns p. 640

10 December 1789. DAVID BATTIN and RHODA LAWRENCE, dau. of Thomas Lawrence. Sur. William Lawrence. Wit. Francis Young, Jr. Married 24 Dec. by Rev. George Gurley, Rector of St. Luke's Parish, Episcopal Church. p. 63

26 September 1782. ABSALOM BEAL and ELIZABETH PARKER. Ministers' returns p. 631

26 October 1808. ARTHUR BEAL and SALLY MOUNTFORTE, dau. of Thomas Mountforte. Sur. Jacob Beal. Wit. Benjamin Cobb. p. 186

7 September 1786. ASA BEAL and FANNY POPE. Married by Rev. George Gurley, Rector of St. Luke's Parish, Episcopal Church. Ministers' returns p. 644

1 December 1810. ASA BEAL and PAMELIA BEAL, age 30. Sur. John Johnston. Married 6 Dec. by Rev. Exum Everett. p. 203

6 April 1801. BENJAMIN BEAL and WINNY JOHNSON. Sur. Eli Beal. p. 144

1 June 1809. BENJAMIN BEAL and EADY CARR, consent of Priscilla Carr. Sur. Brittain Bryant. Wit. James Rochelle and Samuel Kello. Double wedding; see Brittain Bryant. p. 192

2 January 1806. BRITTAIN BEAL and PRISCILLA CARR. Sur. Jacob
Beal. Wit. Benjamin Cobb. p. 168

13 June 1784. BURWELL BEAL and CHERRY WILSON. Ministers'
returns p. 634

20 August 1810. DEMPSEY BEAL and SALLY VICK, dau. of Councill
and Edith Vick. Sur. Thomas West. Wit. Allen Butler and James
Rochelle. Married 23 Aug. by Rev. Benjamin Barnes. Methodist.
p. 202

20 December 1802. EDWIN BEAL and GRACE CRUMPLER. Sur. Benjamin
Beal. Wit. Benjamin Cobb. p. 151

18 March 1784. JACOB BEAL and ELIZABETH DAUGHTRY. Ministers'
returns p. 634

19 January 1801. JACOB BEAL and SARAH PORTER, dau. of Winna
Porter. Sur. Benjamin Beal. Wit. Samuel Kello. p. 142

26 October 1808. JACOB BEAL and PEGGY MOUNTFORTE, dau. of
Thomas Mountforte. Sur. Arthur Beal. Wit. Benjamin Cobb
and Samuel Kello. p. 186

20 June 1803. JEREMIAH BEAL and JERUSHA ROE, dau. of Cordal
Roe who is surety. Wit. Benjamin Cobb. p. 154

15 May 1809. JESSE BEAL and MARGARET P. WHITEHEAD. Sur.
John Beal. Wit. Samuel Kello. Married by Rev. Benjamin
Barnes, Methodist. p. 191

30 October 1783. JOHN BEAL and ISABEL BEAL. Ministers'
returns p. 633

20 November 1809. JOHN BEAL and NANCY FOWLER. Sur. Miles
Fowler. Wit. Harrison Minton. p. 195

19 January 1805. JORDAN BEAL and BETSEY EDWARDS, dau. of
Kinchen Edwards. Sur. Lemuel Joyner. p. 165

31 January 1803. JOSHUA BEAL and JULIA BEAL, dau. of Martha
Beal. Sur. Joshua Joyner. Wit. Samuel Kello. p. 152

24 January 1806. MILLS BEAL and PEGGY COUNCIL. Sur. Joshua
Joyner. Wit. Benjamin Cobb. p. 169

29 October 1789. ROBERT BEAL and HOLLAND BREWER, both of
Isle of Wight County. Married by Rev. D.C. Barrow. Ministers'
returns p. 643

19 December 1786. SHADRACK BEAL and SARAH JOYNER. Sur. David
Wright. Wit. Francis Young, Jr. Married 21 Dec. by Rev.
David Barrow. p. 49

19 October 1778. WILLIAM BEAL and ELIZABETH JOYNER. Sur.
Jacob Joyner. No witness given. p. 27

12 December 1810. WILLIAM BEAL and ELIZABETH POPE, dau. of
Evans Pope. Sur. Joseph Pope. Wit. James Rochelle. Married
13 Dec. by Rev. Benjamin Barnes, Methodist. p. 203

15 February 1787. BENJAMIN BEALE and ELIZABETH COBB. Sur.
James Wright. Wit. Samuel Kello. Married 21 Feb. by Rev.
David Barrow. She must have been a widow as her dau. Rebecca
Cobb married James Brewer 1804. p. 50

12 December 1793. BURWELL BEALE and MILLY BLOW. Sur. Asa
Beale. Wit. John D. Haussmann. p. 92

2 April 1801. ELI BEALE and ANN STAMP. Sur. Jacob Beale.
Wit. Samuel Kello. p. 143

9 October 1797. JOHN BEALE and MILLE BEALE. Sur. Edwin
Beale. Wit. Samuel Kello. p. 115

19 January 1801. RICHARD BEALE and TEMPERANCE BEAL. Temperance
Johnson in consent, dau. of Elizabeth Johnson. Sur. Benjamin
Beal. Wit. Benjamin Westra. p. 142

23 February 1797. SILAS BEALE and LYDIA GARDNER. Sur.
Benjamin Odonilly. Wit. Samuel Kello. p. 114

13 August 1792. JAMES BELL and REBECCA LANCASTER. Sur. James
Lancaster. Wit. John D. Haussmann. p. 83

20 October 1809. JAMES BEN and PEGGY WILLIAMS, dau. of
Matthew Williams. Sur. Richard Buck. Wit. Samuel Kello.
p. 195

21 March 1792. JAMES BENNETT and LUCY SIMMONS. Sur. Samuel
Calvert. p. 81

16 June 1800. SAMUEL BENNETT and KARAN GRIFFIN. Sur. Richard
Rogers. Wit. John Adams and Samuel Kello. p. 136

12 January 1784. WILLIAM BENNETT and ANN JARRELL (on face of
bond Saley on back of bond.) Sur. Henry Blunt. Wit. Samuel
Kello. Ann in Ministers' returns. p. 38

25 December 1788. JAMES BETTS and ANNA CHARLES, dau. of
Matthew Charles. Sur. Micajah Griffin. Wit. Richard Kello.
Married 27 Dec. by Rev. D.C. Barrow. p. 57

30 April 1792. JAMES BETTS and POLLY LEWIS, dau. of Sarah Lewis. Sur. Charles Council. Wit. Willis Woodley. p. 82

16 June 1793. WILLIAM BETTS and LUCY SAVAGE. Sur. John Woodward. Wit. Samuel Kello. p. 90

10 February 1799. BENJAMIN BITTLE and POLLY CAPELL, consent of Stirling Capell. Sur. William Kirby. p. 125

6 October 1775. KIRBY BITTLE and LUCY WESTBROOKE, dau. of Henry Westbrooke. Sur. William Miller. Wit. Samuel Kello, Will Scott and Enos James, p. 23

17 July 1797. ROBERT BITTLE and PEGGY UNDERWOOD. Sur. John Underwood. Wit. Samuel Kello. p. 115

4 August 1800. WILLIAM BITTLE and NANCY HARRIS. Sur. Newit Harris. p. 137

8 October 1789. ARTHUR BIRD (Byrd on back of bond) and ANN BYRD. Sur. James Bird. Wit. Francis Young, Jr. Ministers' returns 10 Oct. Married by Rev. Robert Murrell. p. 62

30 August 1789. JAMES BIRD and SARAH HATHCOCK. Married by Robert Murrell. Ministers' returns p. 646

23 November 1782. BUTTS BIRDSONG and LUCY BLOW. Sur. Charles Bugg. Wit. Samuel Kello. p. 34

8 December 1785. CHARLES BIRDSONG and SALLY EDWARDS. Sur. Micajah Edwards. Wit. Francis Young, Jr. p. 42

9 March 1786. CHARLES BIRDSONG and MILLE DAUGHTRY. Married by Rev. David Barrow, Ministers' returns p. 638

25 October 1800. ROBERT BIRDSONG and PEGGY HINES. Sur. John Hines. Wit. Samuel Kello, Jr. p. 138

25 January 1792. EDMUND BISHOP and ELIZABETH BLOW. Sur. Jacob Lawrence. Wit. John D. Haussmann. p. 78

24 December 1805. JAMES BISHOP and NANNY BEAL. Married by Rev. Exum Everett. Ministers' returns p. 654

27 December 1806. JOHN BISHOP and TABITHA VICK (she has neither parent nor guardian). Sur. Jesse Beal. Wit. Samuel Kello. Married 30 Dec. by Rev. Benjamin Barnes, Methodist. p. 175

7 June 1782. JOSEPH BISHOP and ANN GEORGE (widow) of Nottoway Parish. Sur. John Windham. Wit. Richard Kello. p. 33

15 October 1798. HENRY BISHOP and POLLY EDDERS. Sur. John Phillips. Wit. Samuel Kello, Jr. p. 122

7 February 1789. BENJAMIN BLACKHEAD and MILLEY JOHNSON of Nottoway Parish. Sur. Richard Blackshins. Wit. Richard Kello. Married 19 February by Rev. D.C. Barrow. p. 58

4 March 1789. JAMES BLACKSHIMS and JENNY DRAPER. Sur. Sampson Thomas. Wit. Samuel Kello. On same bond with Sampson Thomas. Married 13 March by Rev. D.C. Barrow. p. 58

7 February 1789. RICHARD BLACKSHINS and LUCY STAUNTON of Nottoway Parish. Sur. Benjamin Blackhead. Wit. Richard Kello. Married 26 Feb. by Rev. D.C. Barrow. p. 58

31 May 1782. BENJAMIN BLAKE and PRISCILLA DAY, dau. of Thomas Day, deceased. Consent of John Adenston Rogers as to Benjamin. Sur. James Blake. Wit. Richard Kello. p. 33

14 December 1783. ISHAM BLAKE and MARY MASSY CLIFTON. Ministers' returns p. 633

13 September 1792. STEPHEN BLAKE and MARTHA BLAKE. Sur. Benjamin Blake. Wit. John D. Haussmann. Married by Rev. Robert Murrell. p. 84

13 December 1787. THOMAS BLAND and MARTHA KITCHING. Sur. Joseph Bradshaw. Married 18 Dec. by Rev. D.C. Barrow. p. 54

-- December 1805. GEORGE BLOW and NANCY BITTLE. Sur. John Barnes. Wit. Samuel Kello. p. 168

15 December 1787. HENRY BLOW and SALLY MYRICK, dau. of Fanny Myrick. Sur. Michael Blow. Wit. Samuel Kello. (Owen Myrick married Fanny Nicolson 9 July 1767. He left a will in Southampton 1786.) p. 54

23 August 1769. JOHN BLOW of Sussex Co. and LUCY BOOTH. Sur. James Booth. Wit. Sam Kello, Arthur Booth, Sr. and Arthur Booth, Jr. p. 14

13 March 1800. JOHN T. BLOW, Jr. and ELIZA ANDREWS. ---- p. 134

20 May 1766. RICHARD BLOW and MARY MOORE (Molly on outside of bond). Sur. James Speed. Wit. Richard Kello. p. 11

20 February 1774. RICHARD BLOW and MARY SCOTT, dau. of John Scott. Sur. John Butts. Wit. Samuel Kello and Edmund Day. p. 20

14 February 1781. RICHARD BLOW and ANN BLUNT. Sur. Benjamin Kirby. Wit. Samuel Kello. p. 29

29 February 1792. SAMUEL BLUNT and ELIZABETH LUCAS. Sur. George Blunt. Wit. Willis Woodley. p. 79

12 December 1757. THOMAS BLUNT, son of Henry Blunt, and ANN GRAY, dau. of Joseph Gray. Sur. Henry Blunt. Wit. Henry Thomas, John Jones and Richard Kello. Consent on same paper with consent for Sarah Gray. See James Wall. p. 3

24 February 1756. WILLIAM BLUNT and MARY PERSON (widow). Sur. Henry Thomas. Wit. Thomas Blunt and Richard Kello. p. 2

4 April 1782. WILLIAM BLUNT and MARY RIDLEY. Ministers' returns p. 361

11 November 1790. WILLIAM BLUNT and ELIZABETH NORFLEET. Sur. John Wilkinson. Wit. Francis Young, Jr. p. 68

13 August 1789. ALEXANDER BLY (Blythe) and MARTHA COUNCIL. Sur. Absalom Joyner. Wit. Samuel Kello. Married 21 Aug. by Rev. D.C. Barrow. (Note: She must have been a widow as in 1794 Mary Council dau. of Martha Blythe marries). p. 61

9 September 1790. JOHN BLYTHE and RHODA WRIGHT, dau. of Joseph and Ann Wright. Sur. Peter Denson. Wit. Absalom Joyner. p. 67

17 January 1794. MATTHEW BOALS and MARTHA WARREN. Sur. John Warren. Wit. Samuel Kello. p. 94

14 April 1791. ALLEN BOON and ANN BRYANT. Sur. Nathan Bryant. Wit. John D. Haussmann. Married 1 May by Rev. George Gurley, Rector St. Luke's Parish, Episcopal Church. p. 73

2 January 1810. BYRD BOON and NANCY EDWARDS. Sur. Matt Boon. Wit. Samuel Kello. Married 28 Jan. by Rev. Exum Everett. p. 197

9 March 1809. DANIEL BOON and LOUISA BOYKIN, dau. of Simon Boykin. Wit. Samuel Kello. Consent only. p. 190

13 December 1794. JOHN BOOTH and TABITHA SYKES, dau. of Ritter Norris. Sur. James Oney. Wit. John D. Haussmann. Married 25 Dec. by Rev. Drewry Lane. p. 99

12 March 1792. LEWIS BOOTHE and CHARLOTTE WINDHAM. Sur. Peter Bailey. Wit. Willis Woodley. Married 15 March by Rev. Drewry Lane. p. 80

1 January 1772. MOSES BOOTH and DIANA MORRIS. Sur. Nicholas Morris. Wit. Richard Kello. p. 17

24 June 1783. MOSES BOOTH and SALLY JONES. Ministers' returns p. 633

21 December 1797. RICHARD BOOTH and ELIZABETH BRITTLE. Sur. John Booth. Wit. Edwin Booth. Married 28 Dec. by Rev. Drewry Lane. p. 118

9 December 1751. ROBERT BOOTH and SARAH BAILEY, (Bayley) spinster dau. of William Bayley and wife. Sur. Moses Booth. Wit. Richard Kello. p. 1

26 June 1781. JOHN BONER (Brier) and SARAH BAINES. Ministers' returns p. 630

WILLIAM BONNER - See William Banner. p. 12

15 November 1806. CALEB BOUSH and SUSANNA SPEIGHT. Consent of John and Elizabeth Vick, guardians of Susanna. Sur. Joshua Fort. Wit. Rice B. Pierce and Elizabeth Moore. p. 174

17 January 1789. WILLIAM BOWDEN and ANNE ALLEN. Sur. Elias Bowden. Wit. James Allen. Married 19 Jan. by Rev. D.C. Barrow. p. 57

21 April 1806. WILLIAM BOWDEN and PERMELIA BAILEY. Sur. Beasant Britt. Wit. Robert Mercer and Bolton Pierce. p. 170

29 December 1790. BRITAIN BOWERS and CREASA LAMB. Sur. John Francis. Wit. Richard Kello. "Briton and Crecy" in Ministers' returns. Married 30 Dec. by Rev. Robert Murrell. p. 69

7 August 1809. JOHN BOWERS and FANNY POPE. Sur. Samuel Calvert. p. 194

28 December 1792. THOMAS BOWZER and ANN MILTON. Sur. Randolph Milton. Wit. Philip Felts and John D. Hussmann. p. 86

21 October 1780. ARTHUR BOYKIN and BETSY BUTTS, both of Nottoway Parish. Sur. Samuel Kello. p. 29

26 October 1782. BRITAIN BOYKIN and OLIVE TAYLOR. Sur. Arthur Boykin. Wit. Richard Kello. p. 34

17 February 1806. BRITTAIN BOYKIN and MARY TURNER. Sur. Howell Beal. Wit. Benjamin Cobb. p. 169

13 October 1785. DANIEL BOYKIN and SARAH BAILEY, dau. of John Bailey. Sur. Hartwell Bailey. p. 42

18 September 1798. DANIEL BOYKIN and NANCY WOMBLE. Sur. Arthur Doles. p. 122

1 February 1797. ELI BOYKIN and POLLY DUGGER, consent of Newet Vick, guardian of Polly. Sur. John Lester. Wit. Samuel Kello. p. 113

13 December 1770. JOHN BOYKIN and SARAH PITMAN, dau. of John Pitman. Sur. Matthew Williamson. Wit. Samuel Kello, Joseph Pope and Jacob Seler. p. 16

16 February 1791. JOHN BOYKIN and DORCAS VICK, dau. of William Vick. Sur. William Vick, Jr. Wit. Samuel Kello. Married 22 Feb. by Rev. George Gurley, Rector of St. Luke's Parish, Episcopal Church. p. 71

4 February 1800. JOHN BOYKIN and JULIA HARRIS. Sur. Barter Taylor. Wit. Eli Eley. Married 6 Feb. by Rev. Benjamin Barnes, Methodist. p. 133

6 December 1791. SHADRACH BOYKIN and SALLY CLAYTON. Sur. Benjamin Branch. Wit. John D. Haussmann. p. 76

8 May 1783. SIMON BOYKIN and NANCY ANDREWS. Sur. John Andrews. Wit. Samuel Kello. p. 36

22 September 1801. SIMON BOYKIN and SALLY CHALMERS. Sur. James Chalmers. p. 146

8 February 1777. WILLIAM BOYKIN and ELIZABETH CLAYTON, dau. of John Clayton. Sur. Stephen Summerell. Wit. James R. Kello, Samuel Kello and Richard Kello. p. 24

2 April 1804. DREWRY BRACEY and MARIAM WHEELER. Sur. John Whitney. p. 160

11 January 1797. JESSE BRACY and MARY DRAKE. Sur. Thaddeus Powell. Wit. John D. Hussmann and Silloisay Bracy. p. 112

15 February 1808. JOHN BRACY and SALLY WRIGHT, consent of John Wright. Sur. Joshua Corbitt. Wit. Benjamin Cobb. p. 182

9 January 1807. JOSEPH BRACEY and MARY JOHNSON. Sur. William Hart. p. 176

20 February 1809. JESSE BRADLEY and ANN J. TAYLOR, dau. of Barton Taylor. Sur. Richard Blunt. Wit. James Rochelle. Married 22 Feb. by Rev. Benjamin Barnes, Methodist. p. 189

15 March 1796. MILES BRADLEY and SALLY BRITT, dau. of Britton Britt. Sur. Joseph Britt. Wit. John D. Haussmann. p. 107

2 February 1790. WILLIAM BRADLEY and ELIZABETH DRAKE. Sur. Jeremiah Drake. Wit. Francis Young, Jr. p. 64

16 May 1808. DIXON BRADSHAW and POLLY JOINER. Sur. Joseph Crocker. Wit. Samuel Kello. p. 185

7 December 1795. ELIAS BRADSHAW and EDITH HEDGEPETH. Sur. Mical Griffin. Wit. John D. Haussmann. p. 111

29 March 1785. JACOB BRADSHAW and MILLE GARDINER. Married by Rev. David Barrow. Ministers' returns. p. 638

4 February 1802. JEREMIAH BRADSHAW and HOLLAND BEAL. Sur. Abia Beal. p. 149

24 June 1809. RICHARD BRADSHAW and POLLY WILLIAMS. Sur. Sion Williams. p. 192

16 December 1796. SEYMORE BRADSHAW and SALLY WARREN. Sur. John Warren. Wit. John D. Haussmann. p. 112

24 December 1791. WILLIAM BRADSHAW and LEVINA JOYNER. Sur. Joseph Bradshaw. Wit. John D. Haussmann. p. 77

20 June 1799. WILLIAM BRADSHAW and POLLY HARGRAVE. Sur. Brittain Travis. Wit. Catharine Travis and Charlot Travis. Married 22 June by Rev. William Hargrave. p. 127

27 September 1771. BENJAMIN BRANCH of Province of North Carolina, and MARY VAUGHAN, dau. of Henry Vaughan. Sur. John Wilkinson. Wit. Richard Kello. p. 17

5 September 1778. BENJAMIN BRANCH and NANCY NIBLET, consent of Edward Niblet. Sur. Samuel Kello. Wit. James Corby (?). p. 27

1 March 1791. DRURY (Drewry) BRANCH and LUCRETIA SUMMERELL, consent of James Summerell. Sur. Benjamin Branch. Wit. John D. Haussmann and Samuel Kello. p. 72

14 May 1767. EDMUND BRANCH and MARGARET DRAKE. Sur. Moses Phillips. Wit. Edward Fisher. p. 12

18 June 1808. EDWARD N. BRANCH and MARTHA JOYNER, consent of John Clayton (For which one?). Sur. Andrew Washington. Wit. Benjamin Cobb and Samuel Kello. p. 185

21 June 1803. GEORGE BRANCH and POLLY WILLIAMSON. Sur. Elias Williamson. p. 155

25 April 1796. GOODMAN BRANCH and SALLY NEBLET (Nebleth). Sur.
Henry Summerel (Summerill). Wit. Samuel Kello and Richard
Kello. p. 108

20 September 1803. JESSE BRANCH and OLIVE HOLDEN. Sur.
William Holden. p. 155

9 March 1809. JESSE BRANCH and BETSEY BRITT. John Urquhart,
guardian of Betsey. Sur. Goodman Branch. Wit. Joseph Britt
and Samuel Kello. p. 190

27 October 1801. JOSEPH BRANCH and MARY ANN BOYKIN. Sur.
Edwin Washington. Wit. Samuel Kello, Jr. p. 147

14 September 1805. JOSEPH BRANCH and NANCY BRIDGES. Robert
Ely guardian of Nancy. Sur. Andrew Washington. p. 167

13 July 1796. PETER BRANCH and PATSY BRITT, dau. of Matthew
Britt. Sur. Drewry Branch. Wit. John D. Haussmann. p. 109

7 December 1779. WILLIAM BRANCH and SARAH DENSON of Nottoway
Parish. Consent of Sarah Denson. Sur. Richard Kello. Wit.
David Benson and Ann Denson. Sarah Denson was dau.of Francis
Denson, deceased, mentioned in his will 1771; mother Elizabeth
Denson. p. 28

19 August 1784. WILLIAM BRANCH and AVEY BOYKIN. Ministers'
returns p. 634

     BRANTLEY: see Brentley

18 March 1805. CORDALL BRANTLEY and PHEBE WESTBROOK, dau. of
Hannah Westbrook. Sur. William Vaughan. Wit. Etheldred Hart.
p. 165

19 December 1803. ELISHA BRANTLEY and MILICENT BUNN. Sur.
Shadrach Cobb. p. 157

6 February 1778. ETHELDRED BRANTLEY and REBECCA PORTER. Sur.
Jacob Newsum. No witness mentioned. p. 25

2 August 1793. JAMES BRANTLEY and NANCY HARRIS. Sur. Exum
Harris. Wit. Samuel Kello. p. 91

19 March 1800. JAMES BRANTLY and TAZZY T. LUNDY, under 21.
Sur. Drewry Bass. Wit. Lunsford Lundy and Mary Lundy, mother
of Tazzey. p. 135

19 March 1806. JOSEPH BRANTLEY and JUDITH McCORMICK. Sur.
Richard Mabry. Wit. Benjamin McCormick, Lunsford Lundy and
Rice B. Pierce. p. 170

17 December 1791. WILLIAM BRANTLEY and SALLY DRAKE. Sur. William Murfee. Wit. John D. Haussmann. Married 25 Dec. by Rev. George Gurley, Rector of St. Luke's Parish, Episcopal Church. p. 76

31 October 1782. FRANCIS BRASEY and FRANCES EDWARDS. Minister's returns p. 631

15 December 1796. JAMES BRATCHER and MARY WARREN, consent of Mary. This is consent only. p. 111

3 January 1787. JOHN BRENTLEY (Brantly) and NANCY ATKINSON of St. Luke's Parish, dau. of James Atkinson. Sur. _____. Wit. Samuel Kello. Married 4 Jan. by Rev. George Gurley, Rector of St. Luke's Parish, Episcopal Church. p. 49

18 October 1791. EDWARD BRETT and SALLY COKER. Sur. Philip Pitman. Wit. John D. Haussmann. p. 75

17 March 1800. JAMES BREWER and POLLY JOYNER, dau. of John Joyner. Sur. Carr Bowers. Wit. Samuel Kello. p. 134

17 December 1804. JAMES BREWER and REBECCA COBB, consent of Elizabeth Beal for Rebecca. Sur. Solomon Cobb. Wit. Shadrach Cobb and Benjamin Cobb. p. 163

29 February 1804. WILLIAM BREWER and SALLY FOWLER. Sur. Jeremiah Bradshaw. Wit. Thomas Standley. p. 159

14 August 1774. WILLIAM BRIDGER and PATSEY BOYKIN, dau. of Simon Boykin. Sur. Richard Kello. Wit. Samuel Kello and Arthur Boykin. p. 21

11 October 1764. HENRY BRIGGS and MARY BLOW. John Thomas guardian of Mary. Sur. John Blow. Wit. Richard Kello, James Vaughan, Thomas Butts and Thomas Barnes. p. 10

10 November 1774. HOWELL BRIGGS and SUSANNA SCOTT of Nottoway Parish. Sur. Richard Kello. Wit. Samuel Kello. p. 22

30 November 1803. BENJAMIN BRISTER and DIANAH SUMMERELL. Sur. Allen Butler. Wit. Benjaman Cobb, Samuel Kello. p. 157

1 January 1810. JOHN BRISTER and DIANA BAILEY. Sur. Samuel Bailey. Wit. James Rochelle. p. 197

12 February 1791. WILLIAM BRISTER and DAMARIS LITTLE. Sur. William Stephenson. Wit. John D. Haussmann. p. 71

9 August 1781. SAMUEL BRISTOE and NANCY WESTBROOKE. Sur. Kirby Bittle and Richard Kello. p. 31

22 September 1788. SAMUEL BRISTOW and MARY CLARKE (Clark), dau. of Rebecca Clark. Sur. William Clark. Wit. Samuel Kello. p. 56

11 January 1796. WILLIAM BRISTOW and POLLY BABB. Sur. John Clayton. p. 105

20 March 1800. ARRINGTON BRITT and PATSEY POWEL. Sur. Beazant Britt. Wit. Samuel Kello, Jr. p. 135

20 May 1803. BEAZANT BRITT and MILLY BOWDEN. Sur. William Bowden. Wit. Bolton Pierce. p. 154

17 October 1808. BENJAMIN BRITT and ELIZABETH HART, dau. of Eliza Hart. Sur. William Joyner. Wit. Samuel Kello and Lucy Hart. p. 186

11 February 1781. EDWARD BRITT and EVERETT MATTHEWS. Ministers' returns p. 630

26 February 1799. HARDY BRITT and PRISCILLA BLOW, dau. of Lucy Blow who consents. Sur. James Blow. Wit. Samuel Kello, Jr. and John Blow. Married by Rev. Benjamin Barnes, Methodist. p. 125

12 January 1809. HARRISON BRITT and NANCY BRITT. Sur. Joseph Britt, Jr. Wit. Samuel Kello. p. 188

7 January 1808. JOHN BRITT and SALLY BOWERS, dau. of Willis Bowers. Sur. Moses Johnson. Wit. Demsey Bowers and Samuel Kello. p. 182

19 April 1796. JOSEPH BRITT and REBECCA POWELL. Sur. John Crumpler. Wit. John D. Haussmann. p. 108

17 February 1800. JOSEPH BRITT and LYDIA BRITT. Sur. Reuben Whitfield. Wit. Samuel Kello, Jr. Married 18 Feb. by Rev. Benjamin Barnes, Methodist. p. 133

16 December 1802. JOSEPH BRITT and SALLY SUMMERELL. Married by Rev. Robert Murrell. Ministers' returns. p. 652

25 April 1785. THOMAS BRITT and SALLY JENKINS, dau. of Spencer Jenkins. Sur. Jesse Jenkins. Wit. Richard Kello. Married 28 April by Rev. David Barrow. p. 40

17 December 1810. WILLIAM G. BRITT and POLLY WARREN. Sur. Cordell Whitfield. Wit. Samuel Kello. Married 20 Dec. by Rev. Exum Everett. p. 203

12 August 1804. JESSE BRITTE and CIDNEY EVERETT, dau. of Exum Everett. Sur. John Britte. Wit. Benjamin Cobb. p. 161

16 April 1804. BRITTAIN BRITTLE and ZILPAH TANNER, dau. of
Darcus Tanner. Sur. Robert Murrell. Wit. Bolton Pierce.
Married 28 Apr. by Rev. Robert Murrell. p. 160

4 January 1794. JESSE BRITTLE and POLLY CARROLL. Sur. Hartwell
Bailey. Wit. John D. Haussmann. p. 93

27 November 1792. JOHN BRITTLE and JANE CARRELL, dau. of
Je-se Carrell. Sur. Hartwell Bailey. Wit. Samuel Kello. p. 86

15 August 1808. MACAJAH BRITTLE and JEASEY BOWERS. Sur.
Willis Dennea. Wit. Willie Francis and Samuel Kello. p. 186

15 November 1799. JOHN BROCK and PEGGY BAILEY, dau. of Absalom
and Helen Bailey. Sur. Benjamin Brock. Wit. Samuel Kello,
Jr. Married by Rev. Drewry Lane. (Absalom Bailey married
Holland Booth 6 June 1780). p.129

14 February 1789. THOMAS BROCK and LUCY GRANTHAM. Sur. Richard
Kello. Wit. Samuel Kello. p. 58

11 December 1786. JAMES BROOKS and HANNAH BALMER. Married by
Rev. George Gurley, Rector of St. Luke's Parish, Episcopal
Church. Ministers' returns p. 644

15 October 1790. ALBRIDGETON BROWN (Browne) and PEGGY RIDLEY.
Sur. Francis Young, Jr. p. 67

18 November 1792. MAJOR BROWN and FRANCES ELLIS. Married by
Rev. Robert Murrell. Ministers' returns p. 647

1 May 1781. WILLIAM BROWN, JR. of Sussex Co. and ELIZABETH
TAYLOR, dau. of Henry Taylor. Sur. Richard Kello. Wit. Robert
Hargrove. p. 30

4 June 1798. ANTHONY BROWNE and ALTHEA DAVIS. Sur. Amos
Brown (Browne). Wit. Samuel Kello, Jr. and Samuel Kello.
p. 121

17 November 1784. BURWELL BROWNE and MARY ANN WILLIAMSON.
Thomas Turner guardian of Mary Ann and is surety. Wit. Patience
Turner and Etheldred Turner. p. 39

16 January 1783. DANIEL BROWNE and PATIENCE VICK, dau. of
William Vick. Sur. James Pennington. Wit. Samuel Kello. p. 35

15 June 1801. JOHN BROWNE and REBECCA JORDAN. Sur. Reuben
Whitfield. Married 26 June. p. 145

24 February 1810. MOSES BROWNE and FEREBA ARTIST. Sur.
Benjamin Whitfield, Jr. Wit. James Rochelle. Married 25 Feb.
by Rev. Exum Everett. p. 199

12 November 1789. THOMAS BROWNE (Brown in Ministers' returns 15 Nov. 1789) and ELIZABETH BRYANT. Sur. Matthew Bryant. Wit. Samuel Kello and Jonas Bryant. Married by Rev. George Gurley, Rector of St. Luke's Parish, Episcopal Church. p. 63

6 August 1798. JAMES BROWNING and TEMPERANCE HINES. Sur. Willis Wright. Wit. W. Evans. p. 122

17 December 1799. BAILEY BRYANT and PHEREBY BEAL. Sur. Amos Joyner. Wit. Samuel Kello, Jr. and William Beal. p. 131

6 July 1803. BAILEY BRYANT and DIZY UNDERWOOD. Sur. Benjamin Johnson. Wit. Bolton Pierce. Married 11 Aug. by Rev. Benjamin Barnes, Methodist. p. 155

7 May 1804. BENJAMIN BRYANT and POLLY STEPHENS. Sur. John Barnes. Wit. Bolton Pierce. Married 18 May by Rev. Robert Murrell. p. 160

1 June 1809. BRITTAIN BRYANT and SALLY CARR, consent of Priscilla Carr. Sur. Benjamin Beal. Wit. James Rochelle and Samuel Kello. Double wedding; see Benjamin Beal. p. 192

17 February 1791. BURWELL BRYANT and SUKEY BARROW. Married by Rev. George Gurley, Rector of St. Luke's Parish, Episcopal Church. Ministers' returns. p. 645

23 November 1803. CHARLES BRYANT and TEMPERANCE BEAL. Married by Rev. Benjamin Barnes, Methodist. Ministers' returns p. 656

17 July 1800. DREWRY BRYANT and SALLY BRYANT. Sur. Ephraim Bryant. Wit. Samuel Kello, Jr. Married 3 Aug. by Rev. Barnes, Methodist. p. 137

13 October 1796. EPHRAIM BRYANT and MILISENT MASSINGALE. Sur. Dan Massingale. Wit. John D. Haussmann. p. 110

5 April 1800. EPHRAIM BRYANT and NANCY BEAL. Sur. Charles Bryant. Wit. Samuel Kello, Jr. p. 135

3 March 1806. JOHN BRYANT and NANCY TURNER. Sur. Lemuel Griffin. Wit. Samuel Kello. p. 169

21 August 1794. JONAS BRYANT and SILVIAH GRAY. Married by Rev. Newit Vick. Ministers' returns p. 650

11 June 1808. JOSHUA BRYANT and SARAH JOHNSON, dau. of Elizabeth Johnson who consents. Sur. Amos Joiner. Wit. Samuel Kello. p. 185

29 December 1806. LEWIS BRYANT and MARTHA WHITFIELD, dau. of John Whitfield. Sur. Charles Bryant. Wit. J.M. Beal. Married 1 Jan. 1807 by Rev. Exum Everett. p. 175

13 August 1789. MATTHEW BRYANT and MILLY WHITFIELD. Sur.
Thomas Browne. Wit. Francis Young, Jr. and Samuel Kello.
Married by Rev. George Gurley, Rector of St. Luke's Parish,
Episcopal Church. p. 61

13 February 1794. MATTHEW BRYANT and POLLY CHANNELL. Sur.
Newit Vick. Wit. John D. Haussmann. p. 95

19 January 1783. WILLIAM BRYANT and RACHAEL DAVIS. Sur.
Nathan Bryant. p. 35

9 September 1790. WILLIAM BRYANT and SALLY BRYANT. Sur. James
Bryant. Wit. Francis Young, Jr. p. 67

27 December 1791. HENRY BULLS and NANCY SUMMERELL. Sur. Boaz
Guin Summerell. Wit. John D. Haussmann. p. 77

10 April 1793. BURWELL BUNN and FANNY WILLIAMS. Sur. John
Lewis. Wit. John D. Haussmann. p. 89

18 August 1777. REV. HENRY JOHN BURGESS and SARAH JONES, dau.
of Albridgton Jones. Sur. Samuel Kello. Wit. Richard Kello.
p. 24

4 January 1775. BENJAMIN BUTTS and BETTY LEWIS. Sur. Benjamin
Lewis. Wit. Richard Kello and Hardy Harris. p. 22

10 April 1783. JAMES BUTTS and FANNY LEWIS. Sur. Thomas Butts.
_____. p. 36

16 April 1810. JOHN BUTTS and LUCY THORP NEWSUM, dau. of
William Newsum. Sur. David Newsum, Jr. Wit. Harrison Minton.
p. 200

20 June 1803. ROBERT BUTTS and ANN E. MYRICK. Sur. William
Myrick. Married 26 June by Rev. Robert Murrell. p. 155

13 January 1783. WILLIAM BUTTS and MARY GILLIAM, dau. of John
Gilliam, deceased. Thomas Gilliam guardian of Mary. Sur.
Richard Johnson. Wit. Thomas Gilliam. p. 34

28 December 1805. WILLIAM BUTTS and WINNIFRED HOLDEN. Sur.
Samuel Kello. Married 2 Jan. 1806 by Rev. James M. Kindred who
says Winefred Holder. p. 168

11 January 1781. ABHEGER BUXTON (Elgher in his signature;
Elijah in tax list), and MARTHA GARDNER. Sur. Simon Murphee
(Murfee). Wit. Samuel Kello. Ministers' returns say Abigher
and 11 February. p. 29

5 September 1805. JOSEPH BUXTON and ELIZABETH HARCUM, under
age. Dau. of William Harcum who consents. Sur. Etheldred
Gardner. Wit. Bolton Pierce. p. 167

9 December 1758. BENJAMIN BYNUM and LUCY WILLIAMSON, dau. of Benjamin Williamson. Sur. John Kello. Wit. Stephen Williamson, John Wilkinson and Richard Kello. p. 5

13 January 1762. WILLIAM BYNUM and MARY CROCKER. Sur. Benjamin Bynum. Wit. Richard Kello. p. 6

10 October 1765. WILLIAM BYNUM and MARTHA CRAFFORD of St. Luke's Parish, dau. of Henry Crafford who is surety. Wit. Richard Kello. p. 11

19 February 1803. AARON BYRD and AIRA TAYLOR. Sur. Burwell Gardner. Wit. Benjamin Cobb. p. 152

12 February 1799. JEREMIAH CAHOON and PHEBE POPE (widow?). Sur. Thomas Vaughn. Wit. Samuel Kello. "Pheebe" in Ministers' returns 14 Feb. p. 125

13 August 1787. GEORGE CAIN and PRISCILLA BASS. Charles Portlock guardian of Priscilla. Sur. Thomas Kirby. p. 52

2 August 1775. JAMES BUTTS CALTHORPE and LUCY BAILEY, dau. of Barnaby Bailey. Sur. John Jones. Wit. Richard Kello, Anthony Calthorpe and Mary Calthorpe. p. 23

6 January 1797. MATTHEW CAMP and PEGGY JOINER. Sur. Robert Council. Wit. Samuel Kello, Jr. p. 112

30 June 1806. MATTHEW CAMP and TABITHA WORRELL. Sur. Reuben Joyner. Wit. Bolton Pierce and Jesse Bracy. p. 171

12 January 1789. THOMAS CAMP and MARTHA WESTRAY, consent of Robert Westray. Sur. John Atkinson. Wit. Samuel Kello. Married 13 Jan. by Rev. D.C. Barrow. p. 57

27 December 1786. JOHN CANADA (Cannada or Cannaday) and SUSANNA TANN - in bond, Elizabeth in consent, dau. of John and Susannah Tann. Sur. John Tann. Wit. Richard Kello and Thomas Tann. Married 22 Jan. 1787 by Rev. David Barrow who says Elizabeth. p. 49

6 April 1808. THOMAS CAPELL and MARTHA KIRBY JOHNSON, dau. of Harris Johnson. Sur. Benjamin Bittle. Wit. Samuel Kello. p. 184

9 April 1795. WILKINSON CAPELL (Capel) and PEGGY BARHAM, dau. of Joel Barham. Sur. William Halliman. Wit. Samuel Kello. p. 101

18 March 1794. JOHN CARSTAPHEN and PEGGY GRIFFIN. Sur. Micajah Griffin. Wit. Richard Kello. p. 96

September 1798 (after 18th). ABRAHAM CARR and MARY JOHNSON. Sur. Pellnay (Pattesay) Johnson. The name of the surety must by Pettway Johnson. p. 122

19 September 1807. ABRAHAM CARR and REBECCA LUTER. Jonathan Luter guardian of Rebecca. Sur. Pettway Johnson. p. 180

18 January 1802. ARTHUR CARR and PRISCILLA WILLIAMS. Sur. David Williams. Wit. Samuel Kello, Jr. p. 149

17 October 1807. BENJAMIN CARR and CATHERINE ENGLISH. Sur. Samuel Corbitt. p. 180

17 February 1785. DEMPSEY CARR and ANN HOLLAND. Ministers' returns p. 635

4 January 1794. JOHN CARR and MARY WOODWARD, dau. of Samuel Woodward, Sr. Sur. Samuel Woodward, Jr. p. 93

20 April 1807. JOHN CARR and ELIZABETH JOHNSON, consent of Betsy Johnson. Sur. John Woodard. Wit. Benjamin Cobb. Married 5 May by Rev. Benjamin Barnes, Methodist. p. 178

7 December 1808. JOHN CARR and SALLY MILES. Sur. Jacob Williams. Wit. Benjamin Cobb. p. 187

15 June 1809. JOHN CARR and MARY A. EVANS. Sur. Thomas D. Price. Wit. Harrison Minton. Married 17 June by Rev. Benjamin Barnes, Methodist. p. 192

15 June 1785. MILLS CARR and HONOUR CARR. Ministers' returns p. 636

11 February 1768. ROBERT CARR and ELIZABETH VASSER, dau. of Nathan Vasser. Sur. John Everett. Wit. Richard Kello. p. 13

25 June 1789. THOMAS CARR of the Isle of Wight Co., and CHARLOTTE BEAL. Married by Rev. D.C. Barrow. Ministers' returns p. 642

14 January 1803. WILLIAM CARRELL of Sussex Co. and SARAH CARRELL. Consent only. p. 152

19 January 1804. WILLIAM CARRELL and SARAH CARRELL. Married by Rev. Drewry Lane. Ministers' returns p. 653

18 March 1794. BENJAMIN CARROLE (Carroll) and POLLY WASHINGTON, dau. of Jesse Washington. Sur. Charles Bailey. Wit. Richard Kello. p. 96

19 July 1750. EDWARD CARTER and AGNES EZELL, spinster. Sur. William _____. Wit. Richard Kello. 1749 on back of bond. p. 1

12 March 1787. JOHN CARTWRIGHT and SALLY BOSMAN. Sur. John Frances. Wit. Francis Young, Jr. Married 15 Mar. by Rev. George Gurley, Rector of St. Luke's Parish, Episcopal Church. p. 51

26 December 1782. MILES CARY and FRANCES B. PETERSON.
Ministers' returns p. 632

31 January 1785. MILES CARY and GRIZZET BUXTON of Nansemond
Co., dau. of Thomas Buxton. Robert Cowper, guardian of Grizzet.
Sur. James Gray. Wit. Richard Kello. p. 40

5 March 1796. SAMPSON CARY and AINGE ARTIS. Sur. Micajah
Jackson. Wit. John D. Haussmann and Edward Tylor. p. 107

3 February 1795. JOSIAH W. CATHON and MOURNING WEST. Sur.
Lazarus Whitehead. Wit. Samuel Kello. Married 6 Feb. by Rev.
Newis Vick. p. 100

21 September 1801. CHARLES CHAMPION and CALLIA (Seley) GILLIAM.
Sur. Randolph Newsum. Wit. Samuel Kello, Jr. p. 146

24 April 1806. HENRY CHANNELL and ALLIA F. WILLSON. Sur.
Jesse Barnett. Wit. Samuel Kello. p. 171

9 August 1792. JOSEPH CHANNELL and PATSY BRYANT. Sur. Thomas
Brown. Wit. Samuell Kello and Charles Birdsong. p. 83

18 June 1798. WILLIAM CHANNELL and FEREBE EVERITT. Sur.
William Ferguson. p. 121

12 February 1802. CHARLES CHAPMAN and SALLY BRYANT. Sur.
Lewis Bryant. Wit. Ephraim Bryant. p. 149

17 February 1789. JOHN CHAPMAN and MARY SIMMONS, both of Isle
of Wight County. Married by Rev. D.C. Barrow. Ministers'
returns p. 642

22 April 1801. THOMAS CHAPPELL and MARY DRAPER. She signs
Martha. Sur. Amos Gardner. Wit. Samuel Kello. p. 144

4 February 1800. WILLIAM CHARLES and EDITH OBERRY. Sur.
Lemuel Oberry. Wit. Samuel Kello, Jr. p. 133

1 January 1794. WILLIAM CHITTY and SALLY GILLIAM. Sur.
Samuel Matthews. Wit. John D. Haussmann. p. 93

4 February 1810. MILES CLAREY and JENNY WORRELL. Sur. William
Clarey. Wit. Warren Murphy and Samuel Kello. Married by Rev.
Benjamin Barnes, Methodist, who says Jency. p. 198

4 September 1786. JAMES CLARK and SUSANNA JOHNSON, dau. of
Simon Johnson. Sur. John Johnson. Wit. Samuel Kello. Married
by Rev. David Barrow. p. 47

10 October 1793. JOHN CALRK and HELEN WINDHAM. Sur. Benjamin Drew, Dickson Kitchen. Wit. John D. Haussmann. p. 91

30 June 1794. THOMAS CLARK and HANNAH ASH. Sur. John Clark. Wit. John D. Haussmann. p. 97

14 November 1785. WILLIAM CLARKE (Clark) and MARY BRISTER. Sur. William Atkinson. Wit. Benjamin Brock. p. 42

12 December 1793. EDWIN CLAUD and ELIZABETH B. DAY. Sur. Newitt Claud. Wit. John D. Haussmann. p. 92

5 June 1789. JOHN CLAUD and SALLY FRANCIS. Sur. _____. Wit. Joseph Gurley and Samuel Kello. p. 60

8 May 1794. NEWIT CLAUD and REBECCA THORPE. Sur. Matthew Figures. Wit. John D. Haussmann. p. 96

19 August 1799. PHILIP CLAUD and SUSANNA NEWSUM, consent of William Newsum and Elizabeth Newsum. Sur. William Kirby. Wit. Samuel Kello, Jr. p. 128

13 November 1760. BENJAMIN CLEMENTS, JR. and ELIZABETH WILLIAMSON, dau. of Thomas Williamson. Sur. Peter Butts. Wit. Charles Frost. p. 6

18 January 1790. GEORGE CLEMENTS and ELIZABETH PIERCE. Sur. Thomas Clements. Wit. Samuel Kello. p. 64

19 December 1797. JOHN CLEMENTS and NANCY ATKINSON. Sur. Timothy Atkinson (Atkins). Wit. Samuel Kello, Jr. p. 118

10 February 1790. RICHARD PARHER (Parker?) CLEMENTS and PALLY BUTTS. Sur. Elias Herring. Wit. Francis Young, Jr. p. 65

22 January 1801. ROBERT CLEMENTS and PATTY ARTIS. Artice in her signature. Artist in Ministers' returns 23 Jan. p. 142

11 September 1782. THOMAS CLEMENTS, JR., b. 5 Dec. 1760 son of Benjamin Clements, deceased, and Eliza Clements, and MARTHA COCKE. Sur. Hartwell Cocke. Wit. Richard Kello, Thomas Clement, Sr., Alline May and Richard Clements. (Note: Benjamin m. Elizabeth Williamson). p. 34

12 December 1783. JAMES CLIFTON and WINNIFRED LUNDY, consent of Wine Lundy. Sur. Benjamin Clifton. p. 37

5 October 1763. SAMUEL CLIFTON, son of Benjamin Clifton, and SUSANNA KIRBY, dau. of Richard Kirby. Sur. Thomas Clifton, Jr. Wit. Edward Fisher, John West and Benjamin Kirby. p. 8

3 November 1803. SAMUEL CO___ and FRANCES BRIGGS. Married by
Rev. Drewry Lane. Ministers' returns p. 653

4 January 1809. BENJAMIN COBB and SUSANNA GOODWYN. Sur. Samuel
Kello. p. 188

31 October 1806. HARDY COBB and HANNAH EVANS. Sur. Solomon
Cobb. Wit. Rice B. Pierce and Fanny Pope. p. 173

22 December 1787. JOSIAH COBB and LUCRETIA EDWARDS. Sur.
David Edwards. Wit. Samuel Kello. p. 54

22 September 1809. JOSIAH COBB and MARTHA COBB. Sur. Kinchen
Cobb. Wit. Harrison Minton. p. 194

14 May 1795. KINCHEN COBB and MILLY COBB. Sur. Josiah Cobb.
p. 101

23 June 1789. LAZARUS COBB and CHASEY EDWARDS. Married by
Rev. George Gurley, Rector of St. Luke's Parish, Episcopal
Church. Ministers' returns p. 644

15 July 1781. MATHEW COBB and ELIZABETH WIGGINS. Ministers'
returns p. 630

15 December 1785. MATTHEW COBB and MARGARET BELL. Sur. Samuel
Browne. Wit. Francis Young, Jr. This is the date on Ministers'
returns. p. 43

21 January 1801. NICHOLAS COBB and MASON GARDNER. Sur. Kitchen
(Kinchen) Cobb. Wit. Samuel Kello, Jr. p. 142

9 March 1799. SAMUEL COBB and SALLY POPE. Sur. William
Pebworth. Wit. Samuel Kello, Jr. and Stephen Pope. p. 126

13 October 1796. SHADRACH COBB and SYLVIA BEALE. Sur. Shadrach
Beale. Wit. John D. Haussmann. p. 110

23 April 1805. SOLOMON COBB and MARTHA BREWER. Sur. Edwin
Beal. Wit. Shadrach Cobb. p. 166

17 August 1789. BENJAMIN ALLEN COCKE and SUSANNAH CRICHLOW,
dau. of William Crichlow. Critchlow in tax books. Sur.
Richard Kello and Francis Young, Jr. Wit. John Smally. p. 61

25 February 1783. HARTWELL COCKE and SALLY CLEMENT, dau. of
T. Clement, Sr. Sur. John Archer. Wit. John Frances and
Samuel Kello. (Thomas Clement, Sr.?). p. 36

20 December 1783. JOHN COCKS of Southampton Co., and JOHANNAH
COPPER(?) of Isle of Wight Co. Married by Rev. David Barrow.
Ministers' returns p. 637

12 March 1789. WILLIAM COGGAN and MARY PIERCE, both of Isle of Wight Co. Married by Rev. D.C. Barrow. Ministers' returns p. 642

17 December 1781. JOHN COGGIN and ANNE BRITT, dau. of Benjamin Britt. Sur. Joseph Britt. Wit. Samuel Kello. p. 32

5 December 1799. WILEY COGGIN (Coggan) and ALCEY JENKINS, dau. of Nancy Jenkins. Sur. William Barrett. Wit. Samuel Kello. p. 130

17 January 1803. WILLY COGGIN and REBECCA WILSON. Sur. Benjamin Wilson. p. 152

17 May 1789. HENRY COKER and SARAH WASHINGTON. Sur. Thomas Hart. Wit. Samuel Kello. Married 5 June by Rev. D.C. Barrow. p. 60

18 November 1783. JAMES WILSON COKER and MARTHA JONES. Ministers' returns p. 633

7 May 1808. JORDAN COKER and BETSY A. WOMBLE, dau. of Jesse and Sarah Womble. Sur. Jonathan Coker. Wit. Samuel Kello. p. 184

7 August 1807. NERO COKER and ZILPHA DENSON. Sur. George Liberty. Wit. Samuel Kello. p. 179

7 April 1778. WILLIAM COLLINS and SARAH EDMUNDS. Sur. Harris Nicholson. Wit. Samuel Kello. p. 26

27 April 1807. DAVID CONGER and ELIZABETH WHITNEY. Sur. Abia Beal. Wit. Benjamin Cobb and Samuel Kello. p. 179

30 August 1796. GEORGE CONNELLY and PEGGY GARDNER, dau. of Ann Gardner; consent of Henry Gardner. Sur. Nat Newsom. Wit. Samuel Kello. p. 109

7 January 1793. JESSE COOK and LUCY SIMMONS. Sur. James Cook. Wit. Samuel Kello. p. 87

2 June 1793. CUDJOE COOPER and JUDITH _____. Sur. Nicodemus Drew. Wit. John D. Haussmann. p. 89

19 August 1786. JESSE COOPER and SARAH APPLEWHITE. Sur. Benjamin Barham. Wit. Samuel Kello. p. 47

24 September 1804. SOLOMON COOPER and JANE CRICHLOW in bond, Priscilla Jelks back of bond, and in consent. Sur. James Crichlow. Wit. Benjamin Cobb. p. 162

24 September 1804. SOLOMON COOPER and PRISCILLA JELKS on back of bond and in consent. Jane Crichlow in bond. Sur. James Crichlow. Wit. Benjamin Cobb. Married 29 Sept. by Rev. Robert Murrell. p. 162

7 January 1808. WILLS COOPER and ELIZABETH G.G. GRAY. Married by Rev. Drewry Lane. Ministers' returns p. 654

18 April 1807. OBED COPELAND and REBECCA STOKES. Sur. Dixon Ferguson. Wit. Samuel Kello. Married by Rev. Benjamin Barnes, Methodist. p. 178

25 June 1792. ELIAS CORBET and SARAH JOHNSTON. Sur. Samuel Corbet. Wit. Willis Woodley. p. 83

23 December 1783. JOHNSTON CORBET and ELIZABETH COFFIELD. Ministers' returns p. 634

15 January 1810. MILLS CORBET (Corbitt) and MILDRED TURNER, consent of Samuel Turner. Sur. Pettway Johnson. Wit. James Rochelle. p. 197

28 January 1786. SAMUEL CORBETT and BEADY ENGLISH. Sur. Jacob Corbett. Wit. Samuel Kello. p. 44

12 December 1801. JOSHUA CORBIT and NANCY LANKFORD. Sur. Carr Bowers. Wit. Jesse Lankford. p. 148

29 May 1783. JACOB CORNWELL and SARAH WILSINSON. Ministers' returns p. 633

19 January 1754. CHARLES COSBY and ELIZABETH WASHINGTON. Sur. Joseph Lancaster. p. 2

16 December 1799. EDMUND COTTON and _____. Sur. John Cotton. Lower left corner of bond missing. p. 130

18 December 1802. EDMUND COTTEN and AVY MAGEE. Married by Rev. Drewry Lane. Ministers' returns p. 653

2 November 1806. EDMUND COTTON and FRANCES BRISTER. Sur. Theophilus Scott. Wit. Goodwyn Simmons and Thomas Westbrook. See Edwin Cotten. p. 174

4 December 1806. EDWIN COTTEN and FRANCES BRISTER. Married by Rev. Benjamin Barnes, Methodist. Ministers' returns p. 657 See Edmund Cotton

7 February 1778. CHARLES COUNCIL and EDY WORRELL, both of Nottoway Parish, Edy dau. of Richard Worrell. Sur. Benjamin Bradshaw, Jr. Wit. Samuel Kello and Samuel Turner. p. 25

12 May 1806. DAVID COUNCIL and NANCY VICK. Sur. Amos Council. Wit. Benjamin Cobb and Keton Pope. p. 171

24 November 1806. ELEY COUNCIL and ELIZABETH DOLES, dau. of
Arthur Doles. Sur. Willie (Wiley) Doles. Wit. Benjamin Cobb.
p. 174

7 February 1789. JESSE COUNCIL and MARY WORRELL. Sur. Charles
Council. Wit. Richard Kello. Married 11 Feb. by Rev. D.C.
Barrow. p. 58

19 March 1804. JESSE COUNCIL and POLLY BEAL, dau. of Patty
Beal. Sur. Britain Beal. Wit. Benjamin Cobb. p. 159

15 February 1808. JOEL COUNCIL and PENELOPE BRISTER. Sur.
John Lowe. p. 182

29 January 1784. JOHN COUNCIL of Isle of Wight Co., and SALLY
JOYNER of Southampton. Married by Rev. David Barrow. Ministers'
returns p. 637

21 January 1793. LEMUEL COUNCIL of Isle of Wight Co., and
DIZA BEAL. Sur. Burwell Bunn. Wit. John D. Haussmann and
Joshua Beale. p. 88

21 December 1801. SCRUTCHINGS (Crutchins) COUNCIL and MILLY
PORTER. Sur. David Washington. p. 148

8 December 1768. HENRY CRAFFORD and ELIZABETH LONG. Sur.
Willima Bynum. Wit. Richard Kello. p. 14

8 September 1768. JOHN CRAFFORD and MARY TURNER. William
Turner uncle and guardian of Mary, is surety. Wit. Richard
Kello and Edward Fisher. p. 13

13 December 1802. WILLIAM CRICHLOW and POLLY SMITH. Sur.
John Crocker. Wit. Benjamin Cobb. Married 24 Dec. by Rev.
Robert Murrell. p. 151

18 December 1797. WILLIAM CRICHLOW and LUCY ANDREWS. Sur.
Francis Hill and James Butts. Wit. Samuel Kello. p. 117

30 October 1799. JESSE CROCKER and POLLY LANE. Sur. Thomas
Wooten. Wit. Samuel Kello. p. 129

7 July 1798. JOHN CROCKER and CHARITY POPE. Sur. William
Hart. Wit. W. Evans. p. 121

13 January 1794. JOHN CROSLIN, JR. and POLLY COTTEN, dau. of
David Cotten. Sur. James Williams. Wit. John D. Haussmann
and Nathaniel Croslin. p. 94

-- December 1785. ARTHUR CRUMPLER and MARY PURSELL. Sur.
Benjamin Crumpler. Wit. Francis Young, Jr. p. 42

21 May 1799. BEASANT CRUMPLER and ELIZABETH WRIGHT, consent
of John Wright, Jr. Sur. John Wright at top of bond; Benjamin
Wright at bottom of bond. Wit. Samuel Kello, Jr. p. 127

16 July 1785. BENJAMIN CRUMPLER and MARY WRIGHT. Sur. John
Wright. Wit. Samuel Kello. Married 28 July by Rev. David
Barrow. p. 41

16 December 1791. JOHN CRUMPLER and MOLLY BRITT. Sur. John
Crumpler. Wit. John D. Haussmann. p. 76

31 October 1791. MATTHEW CRUMPLER and ANN MERCER. Sur. Benjamin
Crumpler. Wit. John D. Haussmann. p. 75

22 December 1787. WILLIAM CRUMPLER and ELIZABETH LAWRENCE,
consent of Henry Saunders. Sur. John Crumpler. Wit. Samuel
Kello. Married 27 Dec. by Rev. D.C. Barrow. p. 54

28 February 1809. WILLIAM CRUMPLER and SALLY TYNES. Sur.
David Tynes. Wit. Samuel Kello. p. 189

18 February 1791. GEORGE CRYER and POLLY MYRICK, dau. of
William Myrick. Sur. Randolph Newcum. Wit. Samuel Kello.
Married by Rev. John Meglamre, Baptist. p. 71

26 December 1805. JOHN CURL and BETSEY DARDEN, dau. of Robert
Darden. Sur. Joshua Gardner. Wit. Samuel Kello. p. 168

26 February 1789. JOSHUA DANIELS and SALLY FULGHAM, both of
Isle of Wight Co. Married by Rev. D.C. Barrow. Ministers'
returns p. 642

23 December 1787. MILLS DANIEL and MARY WHITEHEAD, both of
Isle of Wight Co. Married by Rev. D.C. Barrow. Ministers'
returns p. 640

10 February 1791. NATHANIEL DARRIS and SUSANNA DARRIS. Sur.
Jacob Darden, Jr. Wit. John D. Haussmann. p. 70

29 December 1794. JOSIAH DASHIEL and SARAH COOPER. Sur.
Samuel Moody. Wit. John D. Haussmann. p. 99

31 January 1807. BENJAMIN DARDEN, of Isle of Wight Co., and
TEMPY BEAL. Sur. Benjamin West. Wit. Benjamin Cobb, Patsey
Beal and Thomas West. p. 177

20 January 1800. BENJAMIN DARDEN, of Isle of Wight Co., and
ELIZABETH McINTOSH, consent of Alexander McIntosh and Elizabeth
McIntosh. Sur. Silas Beale. Wit. Samuel Kello. p. 132

8 May 1810. BENJAMIN DARDEN and CHERRY BRACY. Levery Edwards guardian of Cherry. Sur. Kinchen Edwards. Wit. Harrison Minton. p. 200

9 April 1789. HOLLAND DARDEN and PHEREBE DARDEN. Sur. John McCabe. Married 3 May by Rev. D.C. Barrow. p. 59

14 November 1789. JACOB DARDEN, JR. and MARTHA WHITEHEAD, dau. of William Whitehead. Sur. Nathaniel Davis. Wit. Francis Young, Jr. and Jonathan Darden. Married 26 Nov. by Rev. George Gurley, Rector of St. Luke's Parish, Episcopal Church. p. 63

10 March 1791. JAMES DARDEN and ANN HINES. Sur. Jacob Darden. Wit. John D. Haussmann. p. 72

24 June 1784. JOHN DARDEN and MARTHA WASHINGTON. Ministers' returns p. 634

2 February 1793. JOHN DARDEN and ESTHER BARNES. Sur. Jonathan Darden. Wit. Samuel Kello. p. 88

11 June 1795. JOHN DARDEN and CHARLOTTE VICK. Sur. Jesse Barrott. Wit. John D. Haussmann. Married 24 June by Rev. Newit Vick. p. 102

13 November 1787. JONATHAN DARDEN and ESTHER DARDEN. Sur. Elisha Darden. Wit. Samuel Kello. Married by Rev. D.C. Barrow. Returned 3 Jan. 1788. p. 53

12 June 1794. ABSALOM DAUGHTRY and POLLY WILLIAMS. Sur. Arthur Williams. Wit. John D. Haussmann. p. 97

4 March 1787. DAVID DAUGHTRY and AGATHA COUNCIL. Married by Rev. David Barrow. Ministers' returns p. 639

19 January 1801. ETHELDRED DAUGHTRY and POLLY PORTER. Sur. Jordan Johnson. Married 20 Jan. p. 142

7 October 1787. JACOB DAUGHTRY and SALLY PARKER, both of Nansemond Co. Married by Rev. D.C. Barrow. Ministers' returns p. 640

6 May 1784. JAMES DAUGHTRY and AMY HUGHES. Ministers' returns p. 634

24 March 1798. JAMES DAUGHTRY and FARRIBY (Fereby-Pharaby) JACKSON. Dau. of John Jackson. Sur. William Spencer. Wit. Samuel Kello. p. 120

27 November 1809. JAMES DAUGHTRY and JULIA GARDNER. Sur. Jordan Jackson. p. 195

10 April 1793. MILES DAUGHTRY and MILLEY DREW. Newit Edwards guardian of Mille Drew. Consent only. p. 89

1 April 1793. ROBERT DAUGHTERY and TABITHA HATFIELD. Sur. Jacob Bailey. Wit. Samuel Kello. p. 88

2 May 1782. THEOPHILUS DAUGHTRY and LUCRETIA GARDINER. Ministers' returns p. 631

14 February 1760. BENJAMIN DAVIS and WINIFRED CRAFFORD. Sur. Benjamin Ruffin. Wit. Richard Kello. p. 5

15 August 1789. DAVID DAVIS and PRISCILLE GRAY, of Isle of Wight Co. Married by Rev. D.C. Barrow. Ministers' returns p. 642

-- October 1801. EDWARD DAVIS and MARTHA GILLIAM. Sur. John James. p. 147

1 December 1781. EDWIN DAVIS and LUCY BAILEY. Sur. Anselm Jones. Wit. Samuel Kello. p. 31

20 December 1790. JAMES DAVIS and DIANA BRANCH. Sur. Benjamin Branch. p. 69

26 December 1796. JAMES DAVIS and SALLY MOORE. Sur. Thomas Lane. Wit. John D. Haussmann. p. 112

3 January 1800. JAMES DAVIS and POLLY BOYKIN, dau. of Brittain Boykin. Sur. Jeremiah Cobb. Wit. Samuel Kello. p. 132

17 September 1792. JOEL DAVIS and SARAH POND. Sur. Richard Pond. Wit. Samuel Kello and John D. Haussmann. p. 82

29 April 1794. JOEL DAVIS and SALLY POND. Sur. William Wellons. Wit. Samuel Kello. Married by Rev. Drewry Lane. p. 96

6 August 1803. JOHN DAVIS and ELIZABETH LANY. Married by Rev. Drewry Lane. Ministers' returns p. 653

20 July 1807. JOHN DAVIS and ELIZABETH JUDKINS. Sur. Mial Wall. Wit. Benjamin Cobb. Married 6 Aug. by Rev. Drewry Lane. p. 179

13 February 1791. NATHANIEL DAVIS and SUSANNA DAVIS. Sur. Jacob Darden, Jr. Wit. John D. Haussmann. Married by Rev. George Gurley, Rector of St. Luke's Parish, Episcopal Church. p. 70

9 December 1799. NATHANIEL DAVIS and NANCY BARHAM, dau. of John Barham. Sur. Owen Myrick. Wit. Samuel Kello, Jr. p. 130

23 April 1803. SAMUEL DAVIS and MARY JOYNER (in bond). Martha Joyner on back of bond. William Williams guardian of bride. Sur. Benjamin Vick. p. 154

8 October 1810. SAMUEL DAVIS and POLLY JUDKINS. Sur. Eli
Coker. Wit. James Rochelle. Married 9 Oct. by Rev. Drewry
Lane. p. 202

4 February 1794. THOMAS DAVIS and MARTHA MORRIS. Sur. John
Morris. Wit. John D. Haussmann. Married 6 Feb. by Rev. Drewry
Lane. p. 95

19 December 1810. THOMAS DAVIS and ELIZABETH HARRISON. Sur.
William Thorpe. Wit. James Rochelle. p. 204

23 October 1789. WILLIAM DAVIS and CHARLOTTE FRANCIS, dau.
of Elizabeth Francis. Sur. Willie Francis. Wit. Francis
Young, Jr. Married by Rev. Robert Murrell. p. 62

16 October 1797. WILLIAM DAVIS of Northampton Co., N.C., and
SALLY HARRISON, dau. of Henry Harrison. Sur. Willie Francis.
Wit. Samuel Kello, Jr. Married by Rev. Robert Murrell. Returned
26 Jan. 1798. p. 116

5 January 1763. HENRY DAWSON and MARY LONG of Nottoway Parish.
Sur. Jesse Jones. Wit. David Fisher. p. 8

12 April 1770. JOHN DAWSON and MARY EDMUNDS. Sur. David
Edmunds. Wit. Richard Kello. p. 15

16 October 1790. DAVIS DAY and PRISCILLA BLUNT, dau. of
John Blunt. Sur. Samuel Kello. Wit. John Burges. p. 67

9 January 1794. JOHN DAY and ANN BLOW. Sur. Jesse Holt. Wit.
John D. Haussmann. p. 93

23 July 1804. JOHN DAY and HARRIOTT LAMB, dau. of Clarissa
Whitehead. Sur. John T. Vaughan. Wit. Benjamin Cobb. p. 161

10 Septebmer 1795. JOHN DAY and ELIZABETH COOK. Sur. Lazarus
Cook. p. 103

12 July 1762. THOMAS DAY and ELIZABETH FOSTER (widow). Sur.
John Watkins. Wit. Richard Kello. p. 7

12 December 1776. BENJAMIN DEBERRY and ELIZABETH SUITER.
Sur. John Suiter. Wit. Samuel Kello. p. 23

3 August 1786. JAMES DEFORD and JANE LANCASTER. Married by
Rev. David Barrow. Ministers' returns p. 638

2 May 1789. ELKANAH DELANY and MOURNING BAILEY, consent of
Tryal Bailey. Sur. Jacob Bailey. No witness given. Married
by Rev. George Gurley, rector of St. Luke's Parish, Episcopal
Church. p. 60

18 December 1790. ALLEN DELOACH and MILLE ONEY. Sur. James
Oney. Wit. Samuel Kello. p. 69

22 January 1778. BENJAMIN DELOACH and ANN DUNN. Sur. Samuel Kello. Wit. Peggy Kello. p. 25

20 December 1794. RICHARD DELOACH and NANCY POWELL, consent of Joseph Powell. Sur. James Powell. Wit. Elisha Atkinson and Richard Kello. p. 99

6 January 1792. SOLOMON DELOACH and BARBARA SUMMERELL, dau. of Jacob Summerell. Sur. John D. Haussmann. Wit. Elias Love and Hartwell Summerell. p. 78

8 February 1794. SHADRACK DEMORY and CHARLOTTE HICKS. Sur. Aaron Heathcocke. Wit. John D. Haussmann. p. 95

29 June 1809. JOHN DENNEGREE and POLLY B. COBB. Married by Rev. Benjamin Barnes, Methodist. Ministers' returns p. 658

17 February 1806. WILLIAM (or Willis) DENNY and ELIZA TAYLOR. Sur. Henry Blunt. p. 169

22 January 1800. GEORGE DILLARD and ELIZABETH BOYKIN. Sur. William Crichlow. p. 133

26 July 1809. JOHN DOCKERTY and REBECCA M. HOBBS. Sur. Silas Hobbs. Wit. James Rochelle. p. 193

27 December 1790. WILLIAM DOER in bond - WILLIAM DORR on back of bond, and ELIZABETH HATFIELD, dau. of Philemon and Mary Hatfield. Elizabeth called Betsy in consent. Sur. Jacob Baily. Wit. Richard Kello. See William Dorr. p. 69

4 January 1796. ARTHUR DOLES and ELIZABETH JENKINS. Sur. Patrick Gwathney. Wit. John D. Haussmann. p. 105

14 May 1787. HENRY DOLES and RHODE HOOD. Sur. Francis Price (?) (or Penrise). p. 51

7 November 1807. WILEY DOLES and ELIZABETH TURNER. Sur. Silas Summerell. Wit. Benjamin Cobb and Samuel Kello. p. 180

27 January 1809. WILLIE (Wiley) DOLES and TABITHA BRADSHAW. Sur. Benjamin Bradshaw. Wit. Samuel Kello. p. 188

20 August 1804. WILLIS DOLES and POLLY MERCER. Matthew Crumper guardian of Polly. Sur. Robert Stephenson. Wit. Samuel Kello. p. 161

27 December 1790. WILLIAM DORR and ELIZABETH HATFIELD, dau. of Philemon and Mary Hatfield. Sur. Jacob Bailey. Wit. Richard Kello. See William Doer. p. 69

16 December 1809. JEREMIAH DOYAL and LUCY WILLIAMS, of age.
Sur. Miles Griffin. Wit. Samuel Kello. p. 196

24 December 1801. JOEL DOYAL and MARTHA NEWSUM. Sur. Joel
Vick. Wit. Samuel Kello. p. 148

28 January 1809. DAVID DOYALL and TEMPERANCE POWALL. Sur.
Joseph Bracey. Wit. Samuel Kello. p. 188

21 February 1797. DANIEL DOYEL and TEMPERANCE CHAPMAN. Sur.
Benjamin Bradshaw. Wit. Samuel Kello and Joseph Bradshaw.
p. 114

25 February 1794. EDWARD DOYEL and FRANKEY BARNES. Sur. Amos
Council. p. 95

21 February 1803. PHILIP DOYEL and RHODA COUNCIL, consent of
Amos and Elizabeth Council. Sur. Samuel Barden. p. 152

1 July 1786. RICHARD DOYEL and OLIVE JOHNSON. Joseph Vick
guardian of Olive. Sur. Carr Doyel. Wit. Samuel Kello.
Married 3 Aug. by Rev. George Gurley, Rector of St. Luke's
Parish, Episcopal Church, who says Johnston. p. 46

30 November 1796. AMOS DOYELL and SALLY MOUNTFORT. Sur.
Shadrach Doyle. Wit. John D. Haussmann. p. 110

26 March 1801. HARDY DOYELL and MARY HART. Sur. David
Washington. Wit. Samuel Kello, Jr. Doyall on outside of
bond. p. 143

20 March 1801. JOHN DOYELL and DIANA COUNCIL. Sur. Charles
Council. Wit. Samuel Kello, Jr. Doyal on outside of bond.
p. 143

4 April 1801. MILLS DOYELL and DYZA (Diza) COUNCIL, dau. of
Martha Blythe. Sur. John Davis. p. 143

18 March 1799. SHADRACH DOYELL and LUCY DOYELL. Sur. Jacob
Barnes. Wit. Samuel Kello, Jr. p. 126

14 May 1799. AMOS DRAKE and ELIZABETH JAMES, consent of John
James. Sur. Hardy Drake. Wit. William Booth. p. 127

15 February 1797. ARCHIBALD DRAKE and POLLY WILLIAMS, both
parents consent. Sur. Eaton Joiner. Wit. John D. Haussmann.
p. 113

9 December 1789. BARNABAS DRAKE, JR. and KISSIAH TURNER.
Wit. Francis Young, Jr. This is consent only. p. 63

21 June 1791. CORDALL (Cordel) DRAKE and POLLY WESTER, on
face of bond, MARY WESTER on back of bond. Sur. Baker Joyner.
Wit. John D. Haussmann. p. 74

14 May 1792. DRURY DRAKE and SARAH KITCHEN, consent of William and Martha Kitchen. Sur. Jacob Joyner. Wit. John D. Haussmann and William Williams. p. 82

16 February 1792. EDWIN DRAKE and SARAH WHITEHEAD, dau. of Elizabeth Vellums. Sur. Absalom Joyner. Wit. Samuel Kello. p. 79

7 June 1796. HARDY DRAKE and PHERIBY WADE. Sur. Nelson Wade. Wit. John D. Haussmann. p. 108

8 October 1787. JERRY DRAKE and POLLY GURLEY. Sur. Benjamin Edwards. Wit. Benjamin Blunt, Jr. p. 53

17 December 1806. JOHN DRAKE and MARY BRANTLY. Sur. Amos Drake. Wit. Samuel Kello. p. 175

15 August 1801. MARK DRAKE and KATY PITMAN. Sur. Eli Edwards. Wit. Samuel Kello, Jr. Ministers' returns 24 Aug. say Catey. p. 145

21 February 1803. RICHARD DRAKE and PHERABA BRYANT. Sur. Exum Drake. Wit. Benjamin Cobb, Nathan Williams. Married 24 Feb. by Rev. Benjamin Barnes, Methodist. p. 153

30 August 1802. SILAS DRAKE and SARAH BEAL, dau. of Shadrack Bell. Sur. Archibald Drake. Wit. Benjamin Cobb. p. 150

28 November 1810. SILAS DRAKE and POLLY BRADSHAW. Sur. Edwin Drake. Wit. Samuel Kello. p. 203

16 January 1792. SIMMONS DRAKE and LUCY FRANCIS. Sur. Burwell Rollings. Wit. John D. Haussmann and T.W. Clements. p. 78

11 February 1773. WILLIAM DRAKE and SYLVIA KIRBY, dau. of John Kirby who is surety. Wit. Isaac Williams and Robert Jones. p. 19

28 January 1808. ELI DRAPER and HANNAH BRISTER. Sur. Thomas Chapell. p. 182

17 June 1783. JESSE DRAPER and PRISCILLA COUNCIL. Ministers' returns p. 637

18 December 1809. THOMAS DRAPER and POLLY TURNER, dau. of Mary Turner. Sur. Thomas Chappell. Wit. Harrison Minton. p. 196

-- October 1783. DOLPHIN DREW and SARAH RIDLEY. Sur. William Hines. p. 37

18 December 1767. JEREMIAH DREW and MARY PARKER. Sur. Drewry Parker. Wit. Edward Fisher. p. 13

18 February 1781. JESSE DREW and ANN BLUNT. Ministers'
returns p. 630

13 July 1758. JOHN DREW and JUDITH DAVIS. Sur. John Davis.
Wit. Daniel Fisher. p. 4

1 February 1797. AMOS DREWRY and SARAH WELLONS. Sur. Benjamin
Bradshaw. Wit. Samuel Kello, Jr. p. 113

24 January 1807. JAMES DREWRY and FANNY ARRINGTON. Sur. Henry
Arrington. Wit. Samuel Kello. Married 29 Jan. by Rev. Drewry
Lane. p. 176

13 August 1788. JOHN DREWRY and REBECCA DREWRY. Sur. Silas
Love. Married 14 Aug. by Rev. D.C. Barrow. p. 56

6 August 1796. JOSEPH DREWRY and ELIZABETH DREWRY. Sur.
John Pons. Wit. Samuel Kello and John D. Haussmann. p. 109

15 January 1810. JOSEPH DREWRY and BARSHEBA MURFEE. Sur.
J. Bell. Wit. James Rochelle. p. 198

7 November 1798. SAMUEL DREWRY and LUCY ARRINGTON. Sur.
William Evans. Wit. Sarah Arrington. p. 123

8 February 1787. HUMPHREY DRURY (Drewry) and FRANCES SIMMONS.
Sur. John Simmons. No wit. given. Married 15 Feb. by Rev.
George Gurley, Rector of St. Luke's Parish, Episcopal Church.
p. 50

24 August 1778. HOWELL DUGGER of Brunswick Co., and SARAH
VICK of St. Luke's Parish. Son of John Dugger. Sur. Thomas
Vick. Wit. Samuel Kello, James Dugger and Daniel Dugger.
p. 27

30 December 1800. MORRIS DUNN and HANNAH JELKS. Sur. Sterling
Capel. Wit. Samuel Kello. p. 140

30 January 1808. THOMAS DUNN and POLLY BARHAM. Sur. Grey
Dunn. Wit. Samuel Kello. p. 182

17 December 1804. BENJAMIN DONALDSON DUPREE and FRENETTA
TILLAR, dau. of Henry Tillar. Sur. Sterling C. Thornton.
Wit. James Tillar and Benjamin Cobb. p. 163

8 December 1757. HOWELL EDMUNDS, the younger, and LUCY
NICOLSON, dau. of Joshua Nicolson. Sur. Charles Briggs.
Wit. Richard Kello. p. 3

13 August 1789. HOWELL EDMUNDS, JR. and ELIZABETH CRAFFORD,
dau. of Mary Crafford. Sur. William Hines. Wit. Elizabeth
Peebles. Married 15 Aug. by Rev. George Gurley, Rector of
St. Luke's Parish, Episcopal Church. p. 61

17 October 1769. JOHN FLOOD EDMUNDS, of Brunswick Co., and
LUCY GRAY (under 21), dau. of Joseph Gray Esq. Sur. James
Wall of Brunswick Co. Wit. Richard Kello. p. 15

14 March 1776. JOHN EDMUNDS of Northampton Co., N.C., and
SUSANNA MARGET, dau. of Nicholas Marget. Sur. William Blunt.
Wit. Samuel Kello, Jesse Whitehead and John Whitehead. p. 23

18 December 1792. SAMUEL EDMUNDS and ELIZABETH BLUNT.
Ministers' returns p. 632

20 March 1793. WEST EDMUNDS and ELIZABETH JONES. Married by
Rev. John Meglamre, Baptist. Ministers' returns p. 648

11 November 1779. WILLIAM EDMUNDS and MARTHA BRIGGS. Sur.
Samuel Kello. Wit. John Verelly. p. 28

27 December 1799. ALBRIDGTON EDWARDS and ANNE VAUGHN. Sur.
Bryant Westray. Wit. Samuel Kello. p. 131

25 April 1784. DAVID EDWARDS and MARGARET WELLS (Wills).
Ministers' returns p. 634

9 January 1804. ETHELDRED EDWARDS and MILDRED TURNER, dau.
of Jacob Turner; consent only. Married by Rev. Benjamin
Barnes, Methodist. p. 158

22 December 1785. JAMES EDWARDS and MARTHA WILLS, dau. of
Matthew Wills. Sur. David Edwards. Wit. Richard Kello. p. 43

10 December 1789. JAMES EDWARDS and MARY KINDRED. Sur.
Benjamin Kindred. Wit. Francis Young, Jr. and James Millar.
There is a consent dated 28 Dec. 1797, bearing the same names.
p. 63

23 January 1783. JOEL EDWARDS and MARY FERGUSON. Ministers'
returns p. 632

20 January 1762. JOHN EDWARDS and SARAH PITMAN (widow).
Sur. John Crafford. Wit. Richard Kello. p. 6

18 December 1809. JORDAN EDWARDS and KEETEN JOHNSON, dau. of
Willis Johnson. Sur. Jordan Beal. Wit. Harrison Minton and
Samuel Kello. p. 196

26 September 1783. KINCHEN EDWARDS and MIRIAM BRASEY.
Ministers' returns p. 633

21 March 1791. LEVI EDWARDS and CATHERINE TYLER, dau. of
Edmond Tyler. Sur. John Clayton. Wit. John D. Haussmann.
p. 72

10 August 1786. NATHANIEL EDWARDS and MARY COOK, dau. of
Lazarus Cook. Sur. William Vaughan. Wit. Hec. Edmunds,
Francis Young, Jr., Henry Monger, Francis Penrise, Matthew
Joyner and Patience Pope. Married 17 Aug. by Rev. George
Gurley, Rector of St. Luke's Parish, Episcopal Church. p. 46

13 July 1780. NEWIT EDWARDS and CELIA GURLEY, infant under 21,
dau. of George Gurley. Sur. William Edwards. Wit. George
Gurley, Jr., and Jordan Edwards. p. 29

20 October 1800. NEWIT EDWARDS and POLLY DRAKE. Sur. George
Gurley, Jr. Wit. Samuel Kello, Jr. p. 138

20 January 1785. RICHARD EDWARDS and MILDRED WILLIAMSON.
Ministers' returns p. 635

13 December 1796. THOMAS EDWARDS and POLLY STARKS. Gondabel
Starks parent or guardian (Zordabel). Sur. David Spencer.
Wit. John D. Haussmann. p. 111

10 December 1795. WILLIAM EDWARDS and CLOETILDIA COBB, dau.
of Amy Vaughan. Sur. William Lawrence. Seymore Vaughan m.
Amy Cobb 29 Mar. 1781. p. 104

27 November 1804. WILLIAMSON EDWARDS and LUCY JOYNER. Sur.
Lewis Worrell. Wit. Sally Edwards, Benjamin Cobb. Married
29 Nov. by Benjamin Barnes, Methodist. p. 163

2 February 1801. ELI (Ely) ELEY and SALLY JONES. Sur. Richard
Blow. Wit. Samuel Kello, Jr. p. 143

18 June 1798. HENRY ELEY (Elay) and CATEY (Caty) MORRIS.
Sur. Benjamin White, Sr. Wit. Samuel Kello. p. 121

28 November 1805. VICTOR ELEY and RHODA COBB. Sur. Frederick
Cobb. Wit. Samuel Kello. p. 167

1 April 1778. WILLIAM ELEY of Isle of Wight Co., and LUCY
BRANCH. Sur. Benjamin Branch. Wit. Richard Kello. p. 25

25 November 1806. HENRY ELLIOTT and SALLY DAUGHTRY. Derren
Daughtry guardian of Sally. Sur. Henry Hart. Wit. Benjamin
Cobb. Married by Rev. Exum Everett. p. 174

6 April 1792. GERMANY ELLIS and EDITH HARPER, consent of John
Harper and Edith Harper. Sur. John Harper. Wit. John D.
Haussmann. Jarmany on Ministers' returns 8 April. Married
by Rev. Robert Murrell. p. 82

20 April 1791. WILLIAM ELLIS and SALLY MARKS. Sur. Nathan
Marks. Wit. Samuel Kello. Married by Rev. John Meglamre,
Baptist. p. 73

27 September 1787. JOHN ENGLISH and PRISCILLA COFFIELD.
Both of Isle of Wight Co. Married by Rev. David Barrow.
Ministers' returns p. 639

6 December 1803. NATHAN ENGLISH and LYDIA WORRELL. Sur.
John Johnson. Wit. Benjamin Cobb. Married 15 Dec. by Rev.
Benjamin Barnes, Methodist. p. 157

20 January 1800. ETHEDRED EVANS and REBECCA BARHAM, dau. of
John Barham. Sur. Anthony Evans. Wit. Sally Evans and Lucy
Barham. p. 132

21 November 1799. WILLIAMS EVANS and POLLY WILLIAMS. Sur.
Benjamin Evans. Wit. Samuel Kello, Jr. p. 130

5 June 1780. ETHELDRED EVERITT and ELIZABETH MAGET, dau. of
Nicholas Maget. Sur. Jesse Whitehead. Wit. James Maget and
Sarah Stanford. p. 28

28 February 1807. NICHOLAS EVERETT and SALLY EVERETT. Sur.
Patrick Pond. Wit. Benjamin Cobb. p. 177

19 December 1809. SAMUEL EVERETT and BETSEY R. BATTLE, dau.
of Jesse Battle. Sur. Samuel Story. Wit. James Rochelle.
Married 20 Dec. p. 197

12 October 1796. SIMON EVERETT and SALLY FAIRCLOTH. Sur.
William Claud. Wit. John D. Haussmann. p. 110

30 November 1784. THOMAS EVERETT and ELIZABETH ELLIS.
Ministers' returns p. 635

26 November 1782. BENJAMIN EXUM and MARY BIRDSONG. Sur.
Samuel Kello. Wit. Charles Bugg. p. 34

13 September 1759. JAMES EXUM and ANN THOMAS, dau. of Henry
Thomas. Sur. William _____. Wit. Richard Kello. p. 5

8 August 1786. JOHN EXUM and FANNY POPE. Sur. Josiah Pope.
Wit. Francis Young, Jr. Married 9 Aug. by Rev. George Gurley,
Rector St. Luke's Parish, Episcopal Church. p. 46

22 January 1808. ROBERT EXUM and ELIZABETH LOVE, dau. of
Elias Love. Sur. Joseph Bailey. Wit. Benjamin Cobb and
Samuel Kello. Married 26 Jan. by Rev. Drewry Lane. p. 182

16 May 1772. WILLIAM EXUM and MARY THOMAS. Sur. Samuel Kello.
Wit. Benjamin Griffin. p. 18

16 October 1797. JAMES FAIRCLOTH and SUKY STEWARD. Sur.
James Hosea. Wit. Samuel Kello, Jr. p. 116

6 March 1798. MATTHEW FAIRCLOTH and NANCY STEWARD. Sur. James Faircloth. Wit. Samuel Kello, Jr. p. 119

30 December 1773. HENRY FAISON (Faiston) of Northampton Co., N.C., now a resident of Southampton Co., and DIANA GRIFFIN. James Dancy guardian of Diana. Sur. Cordall Norfleet. Wit. Richard Kello, Eaph. Kilby, Henry Nurvell, Edwin Gray and Hurst Line (or Tine). p. 20

16 October 1797. WILLIAM FARGUSON and POLLY GLOVER. Sur. James Daughtery. Wit. Samuel Kello. Married 24 Oct. by Rev. Benjamin Barnes, Methodist. p. 116

19 April 1790. NICHOLAS FAULCONS and ELIZABETH CLEMENTS. Sur. Robert Goodwyn. Wit. Samuel Kello, R. Clements and Polly Clements. p. 65

27 September 1785. BOLLING FELTS and MARY FELTS. Ministers' returns p. 636

8 November 1800. FREDERICK FELTS and BETSEY HINES. Sur. John Hines. p. 139

15 April 1795. FREDERICK FELTS and SARAH HINES. Sur. Etheldred Kitchen. Wit. Richard Kello. p. 101

16 December 1799. HARTWELL FELTS and POLLY CLAUD, dau. of Sally Claud. Sur. Jarrot Westbrook. Wit. Samuel Kello, Jr. p. 130

22 August 1781. NATHAN FELTS and SALLY HARGRAVE. Ministers' returns p. 630

18 March 1792. NATHANIEL FELTS and POLLY REESE. Sur. Phillips Ivey. Wit. John D. Haussmann. p. 81

29 November 1802. RANDOLPH FELTS and HANNAH JELKS, "in her 24th year". Dau. of Kinchen Jelks. Sur. Charles Barham. Wit. Benjamin Cobb. p. 151

4 June 1789. JOSIAH FERGUSON and ELIZABETH WALLER. Sur. Josiah West Cathon. Wit. Samuel Kello. Married by Rev. George Gurley, Rector of St. Luke's Parish, Episcopal Church. p. 60

21 March 1803. WILLIAM FERGUSON and EADY BOON. Sur. John Deakins. Wit. Benjamin Cobb. Married by Rev. Benjamin Barnes, Methodist. p. 153

9 October 1786. JOHN FIGURES and PHOEBY JOYNER, dau. of Joshua Joyner, Sr. Sur. Joseph Scott, Jr. Married 19 Oct. by Rev. David Barrow. p. 48

30 December 1800. DREWRY FIERS and MARY BISHOP. Sur. Stephen
Hancock. Wit. Samuel Kello, Jr. Married 31 Dec. by Rev.
Benjamin Barnes, Methodist. p. 140

13 December 1787. WILLIAM FIERS and ELIZABETH SPENCER. Sur.
John Bishop. p. 54

8 March 1792. WILLIAM FIERS and SALLY JACKSON. Sur. John
Bishop. Wit. John D. Haussmann. p. 80

11 October 1792. JARRETT FINCH and SELAH WIGGINS, consent of
Abram Wiggins. Wit. James Wiggins. p. 85

14 April 1791. JOHN FINCH and SALLY IVEY. Sur. Peterson
Ivey. Wit. John D. Haussmann. Married by Rev. John Meglamre,
Baptist. p. 73

1 November 1806. JOHN FITZHUGH and NANCY HARRIS. Sur. James
Drew. Wit. Rice B. Pierce. p. 173

14 January 1768. THOMAS FITZHUGH and PRISCILLA DREW, dau. of
Newitt Drew, who is surety. Wit. Richard Kello. p. 13

7 March 1806. THOMAS FITZHUGH and NANCY TAYLOR. Sur. Thomas
Ridley, Jr. Wit. Bolton Pierce. p. 169

14 February 1792. WILLIAM FITZHUGH and MARY JONES. Sur. Jesse
Jones. Wit. John D. Haussmann. p. 79

7 December 1801. WILLIAM FITZHUGH, Jr. and CHARLOTTE RIVERS,
dau. of John Rivers. Sur. Thomas Fitzhugh. Wit. Samuel Kello,
Jr. and Charles B. Nicolson. p. 147

6 June 1800. MICAJAH FLAKE and DIANNAH STEPHENSON. Sur.
Nicholas Brister. Wit. Samuel Kello. p. 136

25 April 1782. WILLIAM FLEMING and ANN RAWLS. Ministers'
returns p. 631

26 October 1790. BENJAMIN FLETCHER and OLIVE FREEMAN. Sur.
William Jenkins. Wit. Francis Young, Jr. p. 68

25 November 1799. ENOCH FLY and ALSEA BOON. Sur. James
Sandiford (Sandeford). Wit. Samuel Kello, Jr. Alssea in
Ministers' returns 27 Nov. Married by Rev. Benjamin Barnes,
Methodist. p. 130

3 January 1807. GEORGE FOGG and MARTHA CHAPMAN. Sur. Samuel
Francis. Wit. John Day and Samuel Kello. Married 8 Jan. by
Rev. Benjamin Barnes, Methodist. p. 176

29 February 1808. ZACHARIAS FORGASON and POLLY CRENSHAW, she has no parents or guardian. Sur. Jesse Beal. Wit. Benjamin Cobb and Samuel Kello. p. 183

19 December 1791. JESSE FORT and ELIZABETH HOLDEN. Sur. Richard Marks. Wit. John D. Haussmann. Married by Rev. John Meglamre, Baptist. p. 77

13 June 1793. JOSEPH FORT and NANCY MYRICK. Sur. Arthur Applewhite. Wit. John D. Haussmann. Married by Rev. John Meglamre, Baptist. p. 90

30 September 1809. JOSHUA FORT and MARTHA B. COOK, dau. of Eliza Cook. Sur. James Rochelle. Joshua Fort "of the town of Jerusalem". p. 194

24 February 1787. HAYLEY FOSTER (Healey Forster) and TEMPERANCE BASS. Sur. Thomas Bass. Wit. Francis Young, Jr. and Northington Ellis and Benjamin Hail. p. 50

12 November 1791. MOSES FOSTER and PRISCILLA FORT. Sur. Solomon Cooper. Wit. John D. Haussmann. Married by Rev. John Meglamre, Baptist. p. 76

30 March 1809. NATHANIEL FOSTER and HARRIETT WESTBROOK, dau. of Thomas Westbrook. Sur. Etheldred Edmunds. Married 13 Apr. by Rev. Benjamin Barnes, Methodist. p. 191

22 May 1793. BENJAMIN FOWLER and MILLY WHITEHEAD. Sur. Charles Fowler. Wit. James Chalmers, Samuel Kello. Written Wighthead once. p. 89

13 October 1785. CHARLES FOWLER and CHRISTIAN POPE. Sur. Josiah Worrell. Wit. Samuel Kello and John Crenshaw. p. 42

20 November 1797. EDMUND FOWLER and RHODESIA (Rodia) CARR. Sur. Asia (Abia) Beal. Wit. Samuel Kello, Jr. p. 117

24 November 1806. HENRY FOWLER and CATHERINE BIDINGSTON. Sur. William Pledger. Wit. Samuel Kello and John Vick. p. 175

27 May 1788. JAMES FOWLER and MOURNING CARR, both of Isle of Wight Co. Married by Rev. D.C. Barrow. Ministers' returns p. 641

14 July 1791. JAMES FOWLER and TABITHA FOWLER. Sur. Arthur Williams. Wit. John D. Haussmann. p. 74

17 December 1798. MILLS FOWLER and REBETKER (Rebecca?) FOWLER, dau. of Lewsy (Lucy?) Fowler. Sur. John Darden. p. 124

6 September 1786. WILLIAM FOWLER and MARTHA JOHNSON. Sur. James Wright. Wit. Benjamin Blunt. Married 10 Sept. by Rev. David Barrow. p. 47

17 October 1803. WILLIAM FOWLER and FRANCES BRACER (or Braces)
Sur. Matthew Gardner. Wit. Benjamin Cobb. p. 156

17 March 1783. SAMUEL FRANCIS and SALLY POWELL, dau. of
John Powell. Sur. Nathan Barnes. Wit. Benjamin Blunt and
Samuel Kello. p. 35

4 May 1789. WILLIAM FRANCIS and PRUDENCE POPE, Patience on
back of bond. Sur. Solomon Cooper. p. 60

16 February 1804. WILLIAM FRANCIS and LEVINA WORRELL. Sur.
Joseph Denson, Jr. Wit. Benjamin Cobb. p. 158

8 December 1774. ARTHUR FREEMAN and MARY JONES. Sur. John
Simmons, Jr. Wit. Richard Kello. p. 22

29 May 1794. CHARLES FREEMAN and REBECCAH HART. Sur. Joseph
Hart. Wit. Richard Kello. p. 97

20 February 1804. HENRY FREEMAN and MARY HINES. Sur. John
James. Wit. Bolton Pierce. Married 24 Feb. by Rev. Drewry
Lane. p. 159

4 February 1789. JACOB FREEMAN and SALLY ARTIS. Sur. Nathaniel
Freeman. Wit. Richard Kello and Samuel Kello. p. 58

17 February 1800. JOHN FREEMAN and DIANA SPIVEY (Spyvy). Sur.
William Spivey. Wit. Samuel Kello. "Dinah" in Ministers'
returns 20 Feb. Married by Rev. William Hargraves. p. 134

20 December 1803. THOMAS FRIERS and TEMPERANCE VICK. Married
by Rev. Benjamin Barnes, Methodist. Ministers' returns p. 656

24 October 1792. JOHN FRITCH and JEMIMA BUTLER, consent of
Lewis Butler. Sur. William Clay. Wit. Samuel Kello. p. 85

9 November 1797. JAMES FULGHAM and POLLY HOWARD BRISTER, dau.
of Samuel Brister. Sur. William Clark. Wit. Samuel Kello, Jr.
p. 117

13 May 1788. JEREMIAH FULGHAM and ELIZABETH GRAY, both of
Isle of Wight Co. Married by Rev. D.C. Barrow. Ministers'
returns p. 640

11 October 1799. SION FULLER and SALLY WILLIFORD. Sur.
Thomas Willeford. Wit. Samuel Kello, Jr. and Charles Willeford.
p. 129

22 December 1810. ABRAHAM GARDNER and PEGGY MEALHOUSE. Sur.
Silas Beal. Wit. Samuel Kello. Abraham Carr on back of
bond. p. 204

5 October 1798. AMOS GARDNER and PATSEY DAVIS. Sur. Joseph Vick. Wit. Samuel Kello. Married 9 Oct. by Rev. Drewry Lane. p. 122

16 February 1793. BURWELL GARDNER and SALLY WILLIAMS. Sur. Thomas Combs. Wit. John D. Haussmann. p. 88

-- December 1800. HENRY GARDNER and ____ WREN. Sur. Shadrach Griffin. Wit. Samuel Kello, Jr. p. 141

26 November 1801. JAMES GARDNER and NANCY GRIFFIN. Sur. Samuel Kello, Jr. p. 147

23 September 1804. JAMES GARDNER and SARAH JOYNER. William Williams guardian of Sarah. Sur. ____ ____. Wit. Benjamin Cobb. p. 162

5 March 1803. JESSE GARDNER and SALLY WREN. Sur. Henry Gardner. Wit. Benjamin Cobb. p. 153

17 February 1809. JESSE GARDNER and ELIZABETH VAUGHAN, dau. of Simon Vaughan. Sur. Etheldred Gardner. Wit. James Rochelle and Samuel Kello. p. 189

3 February 1796. JOHN GARDNER (Garner) and PATIA WHITEHEAD. Sur. Josiah Vick. Wit. Patsey Darden, John Darden, Jr. p. 106

24 January 1806. JOHN GARDNER and BETSY PEBWORTH. Sur. Joshua Gardner. Wit. Benjamin Cobb. p. 169

29 November 1807. JOHN GARDNER and MARTHA JOINER, consent of Jordan Joiner. Sur. Amos Gardner. Wit. Benjamin Cobb. Married 5 Dec. by Rev. Drewry Laney. p. 180

28 January 1804. JOSHUA GARDNER and PEGGY DARDEN. Sur. Nicholas Cobb. Wit. Samuel Kello. p. 158

16 May 1803. JASON GARDNER and SALLY MOORE. Sur. Etheldred Gardner. p. 154

1 November 1783. MATTHEW GARDNER (Garner) and ELIZABETH DAUGHTRY. Sur. Uriah Vaughan. Wit. Samuel Kello. p. 37

21 September 1784. JESSE GARNER in bond; Gardner bottom and back, and SARAH SAUNDERS, both of Nottoway Parish. Sur. Westwood Wellons. Wit. Samuel Kello and Benjamin Cocke. p. 38

24 February 1784. JAMES GARRITY and ELIZABETH HALL. Married by Rev. David Barrow. Ministers' returns p. 638

1 October 1789. JOHN GASKINS and RHODA FULGHAM, both of Isle of Wight Co. Married by Rev. D.C. Barrow. Ministers' returns p. 643

21 May 1804. JAMES GAY and PATIENCE DRAPER. Sur. Thomas Chappell. Wit. Benjamin Cobb. p. 160

19 February 1800. JEREMIAH GAY and POLLY BEAL. Sur. Thomas Chappell. Wit. Samuell Kello, Jr. p. 134

24 March 1791. SCHON GAY and SILVYA WASHINGTON. Sur. Charles Bailey. Wit. John D. Haussmann. p. 72

17 May 1794. JAMES GEE and MARY NORFLEET. Sur. Benjamin Williamson. Wit. John D. Haussmann, Susan Drew. p. 97

30 March 1784. WILLIAM GEREY (?) and MARY ATKINSON. Married by Rev. David Barrow. Ministers' returns p. 638

28 July 1806. THOMAS GHOLSON, JR., and ANN YATES, dau. of Eliza Cary. Consent only. p. 172

11 January 1793. JOHN G. GIBBS and SARAH MOUNTFORT. Sur. Matthew Kemp. p. 87

23 July 1782. CARTER GILLIAM and ELIZABETH HANCOCK. Ministers' returns p. 631

27 August 1806. HENRY R. GILLIAM and CHARLOTTE TURNER, dau. of Charlotte Turner. Sur. Peyton Lundy. Wit. Rice B. Pierce and Mary Lundy. p. 172

8 June 1758. JOHN GILLIAM and LUCY CLEMENTS, dau. of Benjamin Clements. Sur. Peter Butts. Wit. Maj. Richard Kello, Benjamin Clements, Jr. and Thomas Clements. p. 4

5 December 1782. JOHN GILLIAM and MARY CHITTY. Ministers' returns p. 632

13 October 1801. JOHN GILLIAM and ELIZABETH ELLIS, dau. of Polly Jelks. Sur. William Myrick. Wit. Samuel Kello. Polly Ellis m. Kinchen Jelk 12 Mar. 1798. p. 146

5 March 1810. MATTHEW GILLIAM and BETSEY BARRETT. Wit. Samuel Kello. Consent only. p. 199

18 November 1782. RICHARD GILLIAM and ELIZABETH REESE. Sur. Joseph Reese. Wit. Anslem Gilliam and Carter Gilliam. p. 34

17 January 1803. ROBERT GILLIAM and MILLEY TURNER. Sur. John Barnes. Wit. Benjamin Cobb. p. 152

20 September 1803. ROBERT GILLIAM and RHODA BRITT, dau. of Nathan Britt. Sur. Newit Edwards. Wit. Benjamin Cobb. Married 28 Sept. by Rev. Benjamin Barnes, Methodist. p. 155

11 November 1790. JOHN GLOVER, JR. of Nansemond Co., and POLLY DARDEN, dau. of Robert Darden. Sur. John Wood. Wit. Samuel Kello. p. 68

10 March 1803. SAMUEL GLOVER and SARAH JORDAN. Married by Rev. Benjamin Barnes, Methodist. Ministers' returns p. 656

18 June 1785. WILLIAM GLOVER and PRISCILLA GREGORIE. Ministers' returns p. 636

1 February 1780. MILLS GODWIN and SARAH BLUNT. Sur. Edwin Gray. Wit. Samuel Kello. p. 28

22 April 1788. WILLIAM GORDON, of Isle of Wight Co., and MARY PARSONS of Surry Co. Married by Rev. D.C. Barrow. Ministers' returns p. 640

23 October 1798. BENJAMIN GRAY and MILICENT MASSENGALE. Sur. William Gray. Wit. Samuel Kello. p. 122

9 April 1789. CHARLES GRAY and ANN BRIGGS, Nancy on back of bond. Consent of Charles Briggs. John T. Blow in same space, probably guardian. Sur. Charles Briggs. Wit. Samuel Kello, James Denson, and Arthur Boykin. p. 59

-- August 1799. JAMES GRAY and POLLY POPE. Sur. Jonas Bryant. p. 128

15 January 1794. WILLIAM GRAY and LYDIA BRYANT. Sur. Jonas Bryant. Wit. Samuel Kello. Married by Rev. Newit Vick. Ministers' returns dated 5 Jan. 1796. p. 94

4 February 1795. MATTHEW GREGORY and REBECCA VICK. Sur. Benjamin Andrews. Wit. Samuel Kello. p. 100

1 October 1792. JOHN GRIFFIN and PATSEY FRANCIS, dau. of Lucy Francis. Sur. Simmons Drake. Wit. John D. Haussmann. p. 84

1 October 1789. MICAJAH GRIFFIN and ELIZABETH WORRELL. Married by Rev. D.C. Barrow. Ministers' returns p. 643

21 April 1806. MILLS GRIFFIN and ELIZABETH CHARLES "with her guardian's consent". Sur. Benjamin Griffin. p. 170

26 April 1785. SHADRACK GRIFFIN and ELIZABETH NELMS of Isle of Wight Co. Married by Rev. David Barrow. Ministers' returns p. 638

20 January 1800. SHADRACH GRIFFIN and NANCY ROSSER. Sur. Benjamin Lawrence. Wit. Samuel Kello. p. 132

24 December 1796. WRIGHT GRIFFIN and ELIZABETH H. SUTER (Luter?). Sur. Turner Newsum. Wit. John D. Haussmann. p. 112

2 April 1791. THOMAS GRIZZARD and MARY SLADE. Sur. Samuel
Slade. Wit. John D. Haussmann. p. 72

28 May 1782. JAMES GROSSWITH and ELIZABETH LAWRENCE. Ministers'
returns p. 631

11 May 1786. GEORGE GURLEY, JR. and LUCY MARTIN, dau. of James
Martin. Sur. William Thomas. Wit. Francis Young, Jr. Married
18 May by Rev. George Gurley, Rector of St. Luke's Parish,
Episcopal Church. p. 46

13 February 1775. HENRY GURLEY, son of George Gurley, and
Priscilla Pittman, consent of John Pittman. Sur. Thomas
Edwards. Wit. Samuel Kello, Edmund Cosby, William Gurley
and Newit Edwards. p. 22

6 November 1797. JOHN GURLEY and BETSEY W. GILLIAM, dau. of
Thomas Gilliam. Sur. Benjamin Edwards. Wit. Samuel Kello,
Jr. p. 116

11 May 1772. JOSEPH GURLEY and MARTHA PETERSON. Sur. Richard
Kello. Wit. Samuel Kello. p. 18

15 January 1789. JAMES GWALTNEY of Isle of Wight Co., and
MARY WHITE. Married by Rev. D.C. Barrow. Ministers' returns
p. 641

5 January 1797. JOHN GWALTNEY and MILDRED LANCASTER, dau. of
Rebecca Lancaster. Sur. James Gwaltney. Wit. John D. Haussmann
and James Delk. p. 112

1 June 1807. JOHN GWALTNEY of Isle of Wight Co., and POLLY
JENKINS, dau. of Valentine Jenkins. Sur. Samuel Davis. p. 179

9 January 1794. JOSIAH GWATHNEY and MILLY RICHARDSON CLARK.
Sur. James Gwaltney. Wit. John D. Haussmann. p. 94

23 December 1771. WILLIAM GWATHNEY and MARY CATHON (widow of
John?). Sur. Thomas Edwards. Wit. Samuel Kello. p. 17

11 October 1799. SOLOMON GWYN and BETSEY BRITT. Sur. Joiner
Waller. Wit. Samuel Kello, Jr. Married 12 Oct. by Rev.
Benjamin Barnes, Methodist. p. 129

14 March 1781. REDMOND HACKETT and JENETETE (or Temble)
FISHER. Mary Fisher mother and guardian. Sur. Richard Kello.
Wit. Richard Kello, Jr., John Carr and Holland Darden.
Ministers' returns say Temble and 25 Mar. p. 30

19 March 1787. THOMAS HAIL (Hale) and MARY DAVIS. Married
by Rev. David Barrow. Ministers' returns. p. 639

31 July 1788. ELIAS HAILE and SALLY STEVENS. Sur. Henry
Love. Wit. Samuel Kello. Married by Rev. D.C. Barrow.
Return dated 14 Aug. p. 55

22 January 1788. JOHN HAISTY and ANGELINA BRADSHAW. Sur. Benjamin Bradshaw, Jr. Married 23 Jan. by Rev. D.C. Barrow. p. 54

18 December 1793. SAMUEL HAISTY and ELIZABETH DREWRY. Ministers' returns p. 634

25 November 1778. GEORGE HALL of Isle of Wight Co. Parish of Newport, and ELIZABETH HAILE, of Nottoway Parish. Sur. Henry Pope. Wit. Samuel Kello. p. 27

21 December 1793. JAMES HALLICOME and MARY BARNES. Sur. Jacob Underwood. Wit. John D. Haussmann. p. 93

21 January 1791. JOHN HALLCOME and ELIZABETH ADAMS. Sur. Lewis Joiner (Joyner). Wit. Samuel Kello. p. 70

7 March 1791. RICHARD LEE HALLCOME and POLLY BROWNING. Sur. John Arrington. Wit. John D. Haussmann. Married 17 Mar. by Rev. George Gurley, Rector of St. Luke's Parish, Episcopal Church. p. 72

6 December 1791. THOMAS HALLCOME and FANNY ADAMS. Sur. John Adams. Wit. John D. Haussmann. p. 76

22 January 1774. MICAJAH HALLEMAN and MARY WILLIAMSON. Sur. Howell Harris. Wit. Joel Harris. p. 20

26 November 1787. JOHN HALLWIN (on top of bond; Hollwig in center of bond; Hillwig on back of bond and in tax books) and MARY EXUM. Sur. Benjamin Ruffin. Wit. Samuel Kello. p. 53

30 January 1778. JOHN HANCOCK and ELIZABETH PHILLIPS. Sur. Anthony Calthorpe. Wit. Samuel Kello. p. 25

31 January 1805. WILLIAM HARCUM and SALLY GARDNER. Sur. Joshua Gardner. Wit. Bolton Pierce. p. 165

5 May 1810. WILLIAM HARDY and SALLY CLIFTON. Sur. Allen Jones. Wit. Samuel Kello. p. 200

16 January 1772. JOHN HARGROVE and ANN NEWSUM. Benjamin Simmons guardian of Ann. Sur. Solomon Deloach. Wit. Richard Kello. p. 17

19 October 1786. WILLIAM HARKUM and TABITHA VAUGHAN. Married by Rev. George Gurley, Rector of St. Luke's Parish, Episcopal Church. Ministers' returns p. 644

19 November 1784. FRANCIS HARREL and LYDIA TURNER. Ministers' returns p. 635

4 December 1804. REUBEN HARRELL and MARY HARRELL, in bond, Mary Beeman on back of bond and in consent. Sur. Elijah Harrell. Wit. Bolton Pierce and Israel Beeman. p. 163

4 December 1804. REUBEN HARRELL and MARY BEEMAN. Sur. Elijah Harrell. Wit. Bolton Pierce and Israel Beeman. p. 163

20 December 1774. ABSALOM HARRIS and ELIZABETH JORDAN (widow). Sur. William Harris. Wit. Edwin Gray, Samuel Kello and Abraham Hargrave. p. 22

8 November 1804. ANTHONY HARRIS and SALLY FRANCIS. Married by Rev. Robert Murrell. Ministers' returns p. 653

14 October 1781. BENJAMIN HARRIS and ELIZABETH MILLER. Sur. John Clayton. Wit. Richard Kello. p. 31

20 January 1801. BENJAMIN HARRIS and REBECCA AVENT. Ministers' returns p. 651

5 July 1781. DREWRY HARRIS and SALLY LUNDY. Ministers' returns p. 630

12 December 1783. DRURY HARRIS and PRISCILLA WAMMOCK. Sur. Hardy Applewhite. 25 Jan. 1784 on ministers' returns also Womack and Drewry. p. 37

11 May 1775. HARDY HARRIS and ANN THORP. Sur. Thomas Fitzhugh. Wit. Samuel Kello. p. 22

14 December 1786. HENRY HARRIS and MARY DREW. Sur. William Weishe (or Wright). p. 49

14 November 1771. HOWELL HARRIS and MARY NEWSON (widow). Sur. James Jones. Wit. Samuel Kello. p. 17

19 December 1779. HOWELL HARRIS and EDITH THORP. Sur. Hardy Harris. Wit. Samuel Kello and Thomas Thorp. p. 28

13 August 1785. HOWELL HARRIS and PHEBE CLANTON. Sur. Benjamin Harris. Wit. Francis Young, Jr., Drury Parker and Mildred Parker. Married by Rev. John Maglamre. Returned 15 Oct. p. 41

11 September 1794. JOHN HARRIS and ELIZABETH HARRIS. Sur. Newit Claud. Wit. John D. Haussmann. Married 19 Dec. by Rev. Robert Murrell. p. 98

13 February 1790. JOSEPH HARRIS and PEGGY LEWIS, dau. of Sarah Lewis. Sur. Hardy Pope. Wit. Francis Young, Jr. p. 65

4 May 1789. LANDON HARRIS and ANN JONES. Sur. Theophilus Scott. Wit. William McEldoe. p. 60

15 December 1804. MATTHEW HARRIS and ELIZABETH WESTBROOK, consent only. Wit. Willie Francis. Married 20 Dec. by Rev. Robert Murrell. p. 163

14 February 1771. NATHAN HARRIS and MARY TURNER of St. Luke's Parish. Sur. John Barrow, Jr. Wit. Richard Kello. p. 16

4 June 1810. NEWIT HARRIS and ELIZABETH BANON or BARROW. Sur. Harrison Minton. Wit. James Rochelle. p. 201

10 February 1763. SIMON HARRIS and SARAH DAWSON, dau. of Henry Dawson. Sur. Chaplin Williams. Wit. Chaplin Williams, Jr. p. 8

21 February 1792. WEST HARRIS and JULIA ATKISON. Married by Rev. Robert Murrell. Ministers' returns p. 646

9 April 1788. WILLIAM HARRIS and MARY MACKEY. Sur. John Carr Staffney. Married 11 April by Rev. D.C. Barrow. p. 55

19 January 1788. ANSELM HARRISON and ELIZABETH GEE. Sur. Benjamin Harrison. Wit. Richard Kello, Rebecca Micklemons and John Micklemons. p. 54

13 September 1792. CHARLES HARRISON and REBECCA JOHNSON, dau. of Harris Johnson. Sur. Claiborne Clifton. Wit. John D. Haussmann. Married 25 Sept. by Rev. Robert Murrell. p. 84

21 December 1795. JAMES HARRISON and TEMPERANCE HART, dau. of William Hart. Sur. Edwin G. Hart. Wit. Samuel Kello. p. 105

20 March 1809. JAMES HARRISON and PAMELA HARRISON in bond, Harris in consent. Sur. Wilkinson Capell. Wit. Samuel Kello and Joseph Stevenson. p. 190

-- February 1786. RICHARD HARRISON and ELIZABETH MOORE. Sur. Thomas Turner. Married 25 March by Rev. John Maglamre. p. 45

-- November 1794. THOMAS HARRISON and LUCY LUNN. Sur. Henry Harrison. Wit. Sarah Harrison. Married 16 Nov. by Rev. Robert Murrell, who says Lucy Lundy. p. 99

4 December 1809. THOMAS HARRISON and ELIZABETH PHILIPS. Sur. Solomon Harrison. Wit. William Harrison, Nathaniel Mabry and Samuel Kello. p. 196

2 February 1804. DREWRY HART and CYNDA HARGRAVE. Sur. Benjamin Brock. Wit. Benjamin Cobb. p. 158

9 January 1805. EDWIN HART and ELIZABETH DAUGHTRY. James Harrison guardian of Elizabeth. Sur. Henry W. Hart. Wit. Bolton Pierce. p. 164

2 October 1803. ETHELDRED HART and LUCY BRANTLEY, dau. of Rebecca Brantley. Sur. William Davis. Wit. Benjamin Cobb. Married 12 Oct. by Rev. Robert Murrell. p. 156

14 October 1788. HENRY HART and ANN CLARY. Sur. Joseph Hart.
Wit. Samuel Kello. p. 56

15 October 1801. JAMES HART and ELIZABETH HARGRAVE. Sur.
Benjamin Brock. p. 146

10 August 1790. JESSE HART and AVERELLA HART. Sur. Henry
Hart. Wit. Francis Young, Jr. p. 66

5 December 1796. MOSES HART and SALLY CLARY. Sur. Anty.
Andrews. Wit. Samuel Kello. p. 111

13 February 1794. RICHARD HART and LUCY CLASEY (Clarey).
Sur. Henry Hart. Wit. Samuel Kello. p. 95

2 February 1788. THOMAS HART and CATHARINE ATKINSON. Sur.
Richard Andrews. (Katharine on back of bond.) p. 55

24 December 1790. THOMAS HART and ZELIPAH (Zeilpah) BOOTH.
Sur. William Spivey. Wit. Richard Kello. p. 69

19 April 1796. WILLIAM HART and ELIZABETH DUNN. Sur. Benjamin
Evans. Wit. John D. Haussmann, William Critchlow, John Lewis,
and Richard Kello. p. 108

24 May 1775. THOMAS HARVEY of North Carolina, son of Benjamin
Harvey, and AGATHA JONES, dau. of Albridgton Jones. Sur.
Benjamin Ruffin. Wit. Richard Kello, James Harvey and John
Harvey. p. 23

15 November 1806. BIRD HARWELL and NANCY BRANTLY. Sur. John
Harris. Wit. Samuel Kello. p. 174

30 December 1772. JOHN HARWOOD of Sussex Co., son of Samuel
Harwood, and MARY (Polly) MURRAY, dau. of Alexander Murray.
Sur. James Jones. Wit. Richard Kello and Thomas Turner. p. 19

29 November 1800. WILSON HASTEY (Haistey, Hasty) and ELIZABETH
WESTBROOKE. Sur. Jarrat Westbrooke. Married 4 Dec. p. 139

20 May 1782. EDWARD HATFIELD and ESTHER BROWN (widow). Sur.
William Stephenson. Wit. Richard Kello. 19 May 1782 Nottoway
Parish. Black Creek Meeting House certificate that have been
thrice published according to law (signed) E. Herring. p. 33

4 November 1804. EDWARD HATFIELD and MASON WARREN. Sur.
Benjamin Britt. Wit. Benjamin Cobb. p. 162

11 January 1793. GEORGE HATFIELD and SUSAN ELLIS, dau. of
Anne Ellis. Sur. Thomas Porter. Wit. John D. Haussmann and
Samuel Kello. p. 87

20 February 1804. MILLS HATFIELD and REBECCA JOYNER. Sur.
John Joyner. Wit. Bolton Pierce. p. 159

10 February 1791. REUBEN HATHCOCK and MIRIAM ARTICE. Sur.
Charles Birdsong. Wit. John D. Haussmann. Married 17 Feb.
by Rev. George Gurley, Rector of St. Luke's Parish, Episcopal
Church. p. 70

18 June 1804. JAMES HEARN and AMY MARKS. Sur. John Phips.
Wit. Benjamin Cobb. Married 21 June by Rev. Robert Murrell.
p. 161

20 February 1804. HENRY HEDGPETH and TEMPERANCE COUNCIL.
Sur. William Charles. Wit. Bolton Pierce. p. 159

21 January 1792. ISAAC HEDGPITH (Hedgepith) and SARAH JOHNSON.
Sur. Basil Hedgpith. Wit. Samuel Kello. p. 78

9 April 1789. JAMES HEDGPETH and JEMIMA HATFIELD, dau. of
Phittman and Mary Hatfield. Sur. John Blow. Wit. Samuel Kello.
Married by Rev. George Gurley, Rector of St. Luke's Parish,
Episcopal Church. p. 59

27 April 1784. MILLS HERRING of Isle of Wight Co., and NANCY
VICK. Sur. Samuel Kello and E. Herring. Wit. William Hallcome.
p. 38

9 January 1766. MILES HERVEY of North Carolina, and ELIZABETH
JONES, dau. of Albridgton Jones who is surety with Allen Jones
of York Co. Wit. Richard Kello. p. 11

15 August 1786. CHARLES HICKS and MARY STEVENSON. Married by
Rev. David Barrow. Ministers' returns p. 639

3 October 1801. LEMUEL HICKS and REBECCA TURNER. Sur.
William Stringfield. Wit. Samuel Kello, Jr. Married 15 Oct.
by Rev. Burwell Barrett. p. 146

1 August 1809. DANIEL HILGERT and MARY (Polly) WILLIAMS.
Sur. Jack Washington. Wit. Henry Lenow. p. 193

6 December 1796. ALEXANDER HILL and SALLY M. WHITEHEAD. Sur.
Maximilion Whitehead. Consent of Miriam Whitehead. Wit.
John D. Haussmann. p. 111

13 September 1786. ISAAC HILL and MILLE HINES. Sur. John
Hines. Wit. Tzd. Edmund. p. 47

2 July 1781. JOSEPH HILL and MARTHA GRAY. Sur. James Morris.
p. 31

10 October 1753. FRANCIS HILLIARD and WINNY HAY, dau. of Peter
and Martha Hay. Sur. Thomas Johnson. Wit. Richard Kello,
Mary Kello, Joel Johnson and Wm. Morgan. p. 1

18 December 1797. BENJAMIN HINES and ELIZABETH SIMMONS WILLIAMS.
Sur. Henry Simmon. Wit. Samuel Kello. p. 117

22 December 1767. CHARLES HINES and ELIZABETH HUGH HALL, dau.
of Hugh Hall. Sur. Abraham Mitchell. Wit. Edward Fisher
and William Hines, Jr. p. 13

3 February 1781. DAVID HINES and ELIZABETH FRANCES, dau. of
Thomas Frances. Sur. John Mundell, Jr. _____. Double
wedding - see John Mundell, Jr. p. 29

21 December 1801. JOHN HINES and SALLY GRESWITT. Sur. James
Greswitt. Wit. Samuel Kello, Jr. p. 148

20 February 1809. LEWIS HINES and SALLY TURNER. Sur. Samuel
Turner. Wit. Samuel Kello. p. 189

9 November 1786. PETER HINES and ELIZABETH BOYD. Sur. Jonas
Edwards. Married 2 Dec. by Rev. David Barrow. p. 48

28 June 1809. RICHARD HINES and DELILAH ALLEN, dau. of Benjamin
Allen. Sur. James Britt. Wit. Samuel Kello. p. 192

12 April 1791. STEPHEN HINES and MOLLY JONES. Sur. Anselmn
Jones. Wit. John D. Haussmann. p. 72

2 August 1806. WILLIAM HINES, JR. and SALLY WILLIAMSON. Sur.
Goodrich Wells. Wit. Samuel Kello. p. 172

21 August 1790. JOHN HIX (Hicks) of Sussex Co., and MARY
ONEY. Sur. Beverley Booth. Wit. Samuel Kello and Francis
Young, Jr. p. 66

21 December 1807. GEORGE HOBBS and ELIZA KIRBY, dau. of
Nancy Kirby. Sur. John Williams. Wit. Samuel Kello. p. 181

11 January 1783. SILAS HOBBS and SALLY STEWART, dau. of
Benjamin Stewart. Sur. Brittain Scarbrough. Wit. Richard
Kello. p. 34

20 December 1800. BENJAMIN HOLDEN and SALLY BUSBY, dau. of
Betsy Busby. Sur. Silas Summerell. Wit. Samuel Kello. p. 140

21 November 1803. WILLIAM HOLDEN and DISY WELLONS, consent of
Westwood Wellons. Sur. Jacob Joiner. Wit. Benjamin Cobb.
p. 157

10 May 1792. WILLIS REDDICK HOLLADAY and MARY FITZHUGH. Sur.
William Fitzhugh. Wit. John D. Haussmann. p. 82

16 July 1778. EVERARD (Everett) HOLLAND, son of Robert
Holland, and DARKEY BARRETT, dau. of Charles Barrett. Sur.
Samuel Kello. Wit. Peggy Kello, William Pierce, Hancock
Barrett and Charles Harden. p. 26

18 November 1797. EVERITT HOLLAND and SALLY LOWE. Sur. John Crumpler. Wit. Samuel Kello, Jr. p. 117

21 February 1808. JAMES HOLLAND and NANCY BEAL, dau. of Asa Beal. Sur. Jacob Beal. Wit. Benjamin Cobb. p. 183

30 May 1785. ARTHUR HOLLEMAN and CATY BRITT, dau. of Edward Britt. Sur. Thomas Britt. Married by Rev. David Barrow. p. 40

14 February 1791. CHRISTOPHER HOLLEMAN (Holliman) of Isle of Wight Co., and MOURNING POPE. Sur. James Clark. Wit. John D. Haussmann, John Carr and William Pope. p. 71

23 December 1801. EXUM HOLLEMAN and NANCY WILLIAMS, dau. of Sarah Williams. Sur. William Deford. Wit. Samuel Kello. p. 148

10 January 1791. JOSIAH HOLLEMAN, son of Jesse Holleman, and NANCY CLARK, dau. of Rebecca Clark. Sur. James Deford. Wit. Samuel Kello. p. 70

9 February 1769. RIDDICK HOLLIDAY and PAMELA RIDLEY. Sur. Nathaniel Ridley who consents. Wit. Richard Kello, Edward Fisher and W. Andrews. p. 14

21 October 1787. CHRISTOPHER HOLLIMAN of Isle of Wight Co., and ELIZABETH INMON? of Surry Co. Married by Rev. D.C. Barrow. Ministers' returns p. 640

7 December 1796. CHRISTOPHER HOLLIMAN (Holleman) of Isle of Wight Co., and SALLY BOOTH. Sur. Benjamin Brock. Wit. Peggy Bailey. p. 111

17 February 1800. EXUM HOLLIMAN and PATSEY FREEMAN. Sur. Samuel Kello, Jr. Wit. Samuel Kitchen. Married 18 Feb. by Rev. William Hargrave. p. 134

26 February 1795. JESSE HOLLIMAN (Holleman) and PATIENCE POPE. Sur. Simmons Gwathney. Wit. John D. Haussmann, Sampson Pope. Married by Rev. Benjamin Barnes, Methodist. p. 100

15 January 1784. WILSON HOLLOMAN and ELIZABETH MOODY, consent of John Andrews. Wit. Capt. Samuel Kello; consent only. p. 38

18 January 1785. SOLOMON HOLMES and NANCY CLAYTON. Sur. John Clayton. p. 39

14 June 1781. ETHELDRED HOLT and MARTHA WEST. Sur. James Doughtry. Wit. Samuel Kello. p. 31

12 July 1787. JESSE HOLT and PHEBE DAY, dau. of Elizabeth Day. Sur. John Mundall. Wit. Francis Young, Jr. and Samuel Kello. p. 52

18 May 1802.   JESSE HOLT and JANE HARRIS, dau. of Elizabeth
Tunnel.   Sur. Holloday Revell.   Wit. Samuel Kello.   Elizabeth
Harris married John Tunnell 25 Jan. 1792.   p. 150

24 February 1803.   JOEL HOLT and FANNY SCARBOROUGH.   Sur. Howell
Scarborough.   Wit. Benjamin Cobb.   Married 27 Feby. by Rev.
Robert Murrell.   p. 153

17 June 1799.   SPRATLY HOLT and ELIZABETH CLAUD, dau. of
William Claud.   Sur. John Wall.   p. 127

8 April 1779.   JOHN HOOD and PRISCILLA GURLEY.   Sur. Elijah
Crocker.   No witness given.   p. 27

4 September 1798.   ROBERT HOOD and MOURNING DELANO.   Sur.
John Jordan.   Wit. W. Evans.   p. 122

30 April 1807.   THOMAS HOSEA (or Hoesa) and BETSY WHITEHEAD.
Sur. Isaac M. Knox.   p. 179

25 February 1783.   JAMES COSBY HOSEE and MARY STEWART.
Ministers' returns p. 632   See Cosby Hosey.

13 February 1783.   COSBY HOSEY and MASON STEWART.   Sur. Benjamin
Stewart.   Wit. Samuel Kello.   James Casper Hosze on back of
bond.   See James Cosby Hosee.   p. 35

18 November 1800.   ALFRED HOWELL and ELIZABETH BLAKE.   John
Blake guardian of Elizabeth.   Sur. William Blow.   Wit. Humphrey
Drewry.   p. 139

30 August 1781.   JAMES HUGHES of Isle of Wight Co., and
AMEY STORY.   Ministers' returns p. 630

21 November 1808.   PLEASANT HUNNICUTT and NANCY BUTTS.   Sur.
Benjamin Hunt.   Wit. Benjamin Cobb.   p. 187

8 September 1763.   WILLIAM HUNT of Sussex Co., and LUCY
WESTBROOKE, dau. of Thomas Westbrooke.   Sur. Richard Kello.
Wit. Edward Fisher.   p. 8

23 November 1804.   WILLIE (Wiley) HUNTER and SALLY LOVE, dau.
of Silas Love.   Sur. Silas Pledger.   Wit. Bolton Pierce.
Married by Rev. Benjamin Barnes, Methodist, who says Willice
Hunter.   p. 163

15 September 1785.   HARRIS HUTCHINGS and LUCY BETTS, dau. of
Banerster Betts.   Sur. Thomas Collier.   Wit. Francis Young,
Jr., John Montgomery and John Meglamd.   Married by Rev. David
Barrow.   p. 41

7 November 1784.   JOHN IRELAND and ANN BARRET.   Ministers'
returns p. 635

18 February 1793. DR. ROBERT IRVINE and LUCY RUFFIN, dau. of Benjamin Ruffin. Sur. John D. Haussmann. Wit. Valentine Jenkins. p. 88

9 August 1799. ADAM IVEY and MARY ADAMS. Sur. John Adams. Wit. Samuel Kello. p. 128

27 February 1808. GEORGE IVEY, JR. and LUCY IVEY. Sur. Henry Ivey. Wit. Benjamin Cobb. p. 183

19 January 1796. HENRY IVEY (Ivy) (under age) son of George Ivey who is surety, and CHARLOTTE GRAY. Wit. Newitt Sammons, Robert Mabry, Hannah Gray and Sarah Drewry. Married by Rev. Robert Murrell. p. 106

14 November 1809. HENRY IVEY and POLLY REESE. Sur. Charles J. Mason. Wit. Samuel Kello. p. 195

9 January 1786. PHILIPS IVEY and SUCKEY REESE, dau. of John Reese, Sr. Sur. John Williamson. Wit. John Reese, Jr. and Samuel Kello. p. 44

13 February 1794. WYATT IVEY and LUCY UNDERWOOD. Sur. Sterling Francis. Wit. John D. Haussmann and Willie Francis. p. 95

17 October 1782. BENJAMIN IVY and SALLY REECE. Ministers' returns p. 631

18 April 1803. JOEL IVY and NANCY JOHNSON. Sur. Benjamin Johnson. Wit. Samuel Kello. Married 30 Apr. by Rev. Robert Murrell. p. 154

22 December 1806. WYATT IVY and ELIZABETH BASS. Sur. Thomas Williford. Wit. Benjamin Cobb. p. 175

19 April 1803. JOEL JACKSON and ELIZABETH CRUCHALOW (Crichlow). Sur. Edmund Burrow. Wit. Samuel Kello, Dixon Forgason. Married 21 Apr. by Rev. Benjamin Barnes, Methodist. p. 154

30 May 1798. JORDAN JACKSON and NANCY GRAY. Sur. James Gray. Wit. Samuel Kello. p. 121

25 December 1809. KINDRED JACKSON and ELIZABETH TAYLOR, dau. of Barton Taylor. Sur. John Bittle. Wit. Harrison Minton. Married by Rev. Benjamin Barnes, Methodist. p. 197

25 July 1795. MICAJAH JACKSON and FANNY BROWN. Sur. Michael Drake. Wit. John D. Haussmann. Married 20 Aug. by Rev. Newit Vick. p. 102

24 December 1795. ENOS JAMES and PRISCILLA VICK, grand-dau. of Nancy Porter. Sur. John Tunnell. Wit. Richard Kello. Married 26 Dec. by Rev. Robert Murrell. p. 105

26 January 1801. JOHN JAMES and NANCY HINES. Sur. Isaac Hill.
Wit. Samuel Kello, Jr., John Hines, and Robert Birdsong. p. 142

9 February 1764. BENJAMIN JARRELL and MARY JONES, dau. of
Albridgton Jones. Sur. Charles Simmons. Wit. Richard Kello.
p. 9

14 February 1752. THOMAS JARRELL and ELIZABETH THORP, dau.
of Timothy Thorp. Sur. James Jones. p. 1

13 January 1774. THOMAS JARRELL and SARAH MOORE. Sur. Henry
Taylor. Wit. Richard Kello. p. 20

12 March 1798. KINCHEN JELK and POLLY ELLIS. Sur. Samuel
Kello, Jr. Wit. Benjamin Johnson. Polly Ellis must have been
a widow because on 13 Oct. 1801 Elizabeth Ellis, dau. of Polly
Jelks married John Gilliam. p. 120

1 May 1793. ABRAHAM JENKINS and ANN OBERRY. Sur. Drury
Williams. Wit. John D. Haussmann. Absalom Joyner. p. 89

20 September 1800. BENJAMIN JENKINS and PATIENCE KITCHEN on
face of bond; Patients Kitchings in consent. Wit. Elisha
Lewis, Martha H. Moore and David Turner. Sur. Samuel Kello.
p. 138

15 January 1791. JESSE JENKINS and NANCY FLETCHER. Sur.
William Jenkins. p. 70

6 October 1777. VALENTINE JENKINS, son of Edmund Jenkins, and
BARBARA BAILEY. Sur. Hartwell Bailey. Wit. James R. Kello
and Robert Williamson. p. 24

1 April 1807. WILLIE JENKINS and ELIZABETH LOWE. Sur. Elias
Lowe. Wit. Samuel Kello. p. 178

23 January 1809. AARON JOHNSON and NANCY POPE. Sur. Jacob
Williams. Wit. Samuel Kello and Rhoda Pope. Married by Rev.
Benjamin Barnes, Methodist. p. 188

5 May 1789. ALLEN JOHNSON and MARTHA LITTLE, both of Isle of
Wight Co. Married by Rev. D.C. Barrow. Ministers' returns
p. 642

18 May 1793. ALLEN JOHNSON and ELIZABETH MERCER. Sur. Matthew
Crumpler. Wit. John D. Haussmann. p. 89

22 March 1789. BENJAMIN JOHNSON and MARY WALLER, dau. of
Winifred Waller; Arthur Waller grandfather of Mary. Sur.
Joel Vick. Wit. Samuel Kello, John Cooper and Benjamin Barham.
p. 59

27 October 1789. BENJAMIN JOHNSON and MARY JOHNSON. D.C.
Barrow guardian of Benjamin. Mary Johnson mother of Mary. Sur.
William Mackey. Wit. Samuel Kello. Married 4 Nov. by Rev. D.C.
Barrow. p. 62

13 May 1808. BENJAMIN JOHNSON and SALLY HARGRAVE. Sur. John
Johnson. Wit. Samuel Kello. p. 184

23 October 1787. DAVID JOHNSON and SARAH BOWERS. Sur. James
Wright. Wit. George Blunt. Married 25 Oct. by Rev. D.C.
Barrow. p. 53

28 August 1800. DAVID JOHNSON and POLLY BEAL. Sur. Kinchin
Edwards. Wit. Samuel Kello, Jr. p. 138

23 February 1792. DEMCY (Dempsey) JOHNSON and SALLY OBERRY,
dau. of John Oberry. Sur. Jesse Council. Wit. Willis Woodly.
p. 79

8 March 1792. ELIJAH JOHNSON and SALLY WILLIAMS. Sur. Stephen
Landford. Wit. John D. Haussmann. p. 80

12 January 1787. JACOB JOHNSON and PATIENCE BRACY, Johnston and
Brasey in ministers' returns, 18 Jan. 1787. Patience dau. of
Mary Bracy. Sur. Kinchen Edwards. Married by Rev. George
Gurley, Rector of St. Luke's Parish, Episcopal Church. p. 49

13 June 1795. JAMES JOHNSON and HANNAH BRANCH. Sur. George
Branch. Wit. Richard Kello. p. 102

18 November 1799. JAMES JOHNSON, JR. and POLLY SUMMERELL.
Sur. Jacob Turner. Wit. Samuel Kello, Jr. p. 129

27 November 1786. JOHN JOHNSON and MOURNING REVILL. Sur.
Etheldred Holt. Wit. Francis Young, Jr. Married 1 Dec. by
Rev. George Gurley, Rector of St. Luke's Parish, Episcopal
Church. p. 48

17 April 1787. JOHN JOHNSON and MARY LANKFORD. Married by
Rev. David Barrow. Ministers' returns p. 639

6 January 1792. JOHN JOHNSON and LUCY JONES. Sur. Nelson
Johnson. Wit. Samuel Kello. p. 77

4 March 1795. JOHN JOHNSON and SALLY ENGLISH. Sur. Jordan
Johnson. Wit. Samuel Kello. Married 2 Apr. by Rev. Benjamin
Barnes, Methodist. p. 100

20 March 1797. JOHN JOHNSON and POLLY HARGRAVE. Sur. John
Whitfield. Wit. John D. Haussmann. Married 23 Mar. by Rev.
Benjamin Barnes, Methodist. p. 114

12 June 1805. JOHN JOHNSON and SALLY DUCK. Sur. Benjamin
Wilson. Wit. Bolton Pierce. p. 166

30 December 1809. JOHN JOHNSON and PATSEY BARRETT. Sur. Jodan
Johnson. Wit. James Rochelle. Married 7 Jan. 1810 by Rev.
Benjamin Barnes, Methodist. p. 197

27 April 1810. JOHN JOHNSON and CHASTITY JOHNSON. Sur. Henry Lenow (Lenoe in tax books). Wit. Samuel Kello. p. 200

6 November 1783. JORDAN JOHNSON and LUCY HINES. Ministers' returns p. 633

13 August 1795. JORDAN JOHNSON and NANNY STOREY (Nanny Johnson on back of bond.) Sur. John Johnson. Wit. John D. Haussmann. p. 103

5 May 1804. JORDAN JOHNSON and PATIENCE MIALS. Sur. Frederick Mials. Married 7 June by Rev. Benjamin Barnes, Methodist. p. 160

29 October 1794. MATTHEW JOHNSON and SALLY WASHINGTON, dau. of Jorg Washington. Sur. Shadrack Doyle. Wit. Samuel Kello. p. 98

3 February 1806. MATTHEW JOHNSON and MARTHA HOWELL. Joshua Howell guardian of Martha. Sur. Jesse Claud. Wit. Bolton Pierce. p. 169

3 February 1786. MOSES JOHNSON and SALLY GAY, dau. of William Gay. Sur. Levi Lowe. Wit. Francis Young, Jr. and Samuel Kello. Married 7 Feb. by Rev. David Barrow. p. 44

14 January 1806. MOSES JOHNSON and POLLY BRITT. Sur. Harrod Summerell. Wit. Colin Kitchen. p. 168

6 January 1792. NELSON JOHNSON and MILLE (Milly) SPEED, underage, consent of her mother Anne Speed. Sur. John Johnson. Wit. Samuel Kello. p. 77

25 September 1806. PETER JOHNSON and ABIGAIL BLYTHE, dau. of Elizabeth Bligh. Sur. Nathan Johnson. Wit. Samuel Kello, J. Williams and Ro. Denson. p. 173

28 October 1793. PETTAWAY JOHNSON and JULIA HARE. Sur. Samuel Corbitt. Wit. John D. Haussmann and Julia Corbitt. p. 91

15 February 1808. PETTWAY JOHNSON and MILDRED GAY. Sur. Joel Council. Wit. Benjamin Cobb. p. 182

11 February 1762. RICHARD JOHNSON and LUCY GILLIAM. Sur. Thomas Gilliam. Wit. Richard Kello. p. 7

21 August 1788. RICHARD JOHNSON and SARAH SPEED, dau. Robert Speed. Sur. Nelson Johnson. Wit. Richard Kello. p. 56

16 April 1795. SAMUEL JOHNSON and REBECCA CLARK, dau. of Rebecca Clark. Sur. James Clark. Wit. John D. Haussmann and William Clark. p. 101

16 June 1790. STEPHEN JOHNSON and SARAH DOYELL. Sur. Jacob Barnes. Wit. Thomas Hunt. p. 65

9 December 1805. STEPHEN JOHNSON and DIZA OBERRY. Sur. Thomas Nelms. Wit. Samuel Kello. p. 168

18 September 1788. WILLIS JOHNSON and LILLEY BUTLER, both of Isle of Wight Co. Married by Rev. D.C. Barrow. Ministers' returns p. 641

22 November 1808. BENJAMIN W. JOHNSTON and ELIZABETH BLUNT. Sur. James Trezevant. Wit. Samuel Kello. p. 187

24 January 1782. JACOB JOHNSTON and MILLY WILLIAMS. Ministers' returns p. 631

19 March 1803. LEWIS JOHNSTON and ELIZA BOWEN, dau. of Arthur Bowen. Sur. Jacob Turner. p. 153

15 February 1785. RAWLES JOHNSTON and PATTY JOHNSTON. Ministers' returns p. 635

5 April 1792. THOMAS (Tommey) JOHNSTON and SUCKY DRAKE, consent of John Drake and Judith Drake. Sur. Absalom Joyner. Wit. John D. Haussmann. p. 81

15 February 1797. EATON JOINER and REBEKAH JOHNSON, both parents consent. On same bond with Archibald Drake. p. 113

16 January 1809. ELEY (Eli) JOINER and NANCY VICK, dau. of Pherby Vick. Sur. Jordan Beal. p. 188

12 April 1792. GILES JOINER and ELIZABETH MARY ANN CHEATHAM, dau. of Archer Cheatham. Sur. Joseph Gurley. Wit. John Cheatham. p. 82

1 February 1809. JOSEPH JOINER and RHODA JOINER, dau. of Margaret Joiner. Sur. Lemuel Joiner. Wit. James Rochelle. p. 189

30 August 1790. KEMP JOINER and SALLY ROLLINGS. Sur. Burwell Rollings. p. 66

13 January 1806. LEMUEL JOINER and SALLY BEAL, dau. of William Beal. Sur. Amos Joyner. Wit. Bolton Pierce. p. 168

19 February 1770. ABINGTON JONES and MARY SIMMONS (widow). Sur. Richard Kello. Wit. John Simmons and Jacob Johnson. Could this be Albridgton Jones? p. 15

22 December 1784. MAJ. ALBRIDGTON JONES and FANNY CALVERT, dau. of Christopher Calvert. Sur. Jeremiah Tyler. p. 39

27 February 1795. COL. ALBRIDGTON JONES and POLLY CALVERT.
Sur. Matthew Calvert. Wit. John D. Haussmann. p. 100

12 February 1801. ALLEN JONES and GINNETT CLIFTON. Sur.
Francis Cordall. Wit. Etheldred Murrell. Married 24 Feb.
p. 143

11 December 1793. ANSELMN JONES and DELILAH SEYBURN. Sur.
William Jones. Wit. John D. Haussmann. p. 92

16 January 1804. BENJAMIN JONES and PATSEY TURNER, dau. of
Jacob Turner, Sr. Sur. Benjamin Griffin. Wit. Benjamin Cobb.
p. 158

13 February 1797. CHARLES B. JONES and SARAH NORFLEET, consent
of John Wilkinson uncle of Sally Norfleet. Sur. Thomas Jones.
Wit. Aug. B. Cocke. (Note: Cordall Norfleet m. Mary Wilkinson
2 July 1771, dau. of John Wilkinson. He died 1788). p. 113

4 August 1797. GEORGE H. JONES and ELIZABETH WRIGHT. Sur.
John Wright. Wit. Samuel Kello. p. 115

4 October 1758. HARWOOD JONES of North Carolina, and ELIZABETH
JARRELL. Henry Thomas Guardian of Elizabeth. Sur. Richard
Ricks. Wit. John Kello. p. 4

11 October 1796. HENRY JONES and ELIZABETH VICK. Sur. Arthur
Bowing. Wit. Samuel Kello. p. 110

29 July 1800. HENRY G. JONES and LUCY WALLER. Sur. Jacob
Barnes. Married 31 July by Rev. Benjamin Barnes, Methodist.
p. 137

18 December 1783. HOWEL JONES and ELIZABETH BOOTHE. Ministers'
returns p. 634

26 April 1764. JAMES JONES and MARTHA THORPE (widow). Sur.
William Fanning. Wit. Richard Kello. p. 9

14 July 1774. JAMES JONES and ANNE VASSER, dau. of Lydia
Vasser. Sur. Samuel Kello. Wit. James Ridley and Abraham
Mitchell. Lydia Vasser was widow of Nathan Vasser. Ann
Vasser mentioned in her father's will 1769. p. 21

18 April 1780. JAMES JONES and AVERILLA SEBRELL. Sur. Anselm
Jones. Wit. Samuel Kello. p. 28

20 February 1786. JAMES JONES and LUCY ONEY. Sur. Thomas
Oney. Wit. Francis Young, Jr. Married 2 March by Rev. David
Barrow. p. 44

9 March 1808. JAMES JONES and CATHARINE WOODARD. Sur. Benjamin
Griffin. Wit. Benjamin Cobb. p. 183

27 February 1788. JOHN JONES and NANCY TURNER. Sur. Arthur Turner. Wit. Samuel Kello. p. 55

1 February 1790. JOHN JONES and PARTHENIA JOHNSON. Sur. Anselmn Jones. Wit. Samuel Kello. p. 64

26 September 1781. JORDAN JONES and SALLY JOHNSON. Sur. Anselem Jones. Wit. Samuel Kello. Ministers' returns say Johnston and 3 Oct. 1781. p. 31

17 December 1810. LITTLEBERRY JONES and TABITHA TRAVIS, dau. of James and Lucy West. Sur. Edwin Travis. Wit. Harrison Minton. James West m. Lucy Travis 3 Nov. 1800. p. 204

16 July 1810. LUTON JONES and CHERRY BRITT, dau. of Nathan Britt. Sur. Reuben Whitfield. Wit. Harrison Minton. Married 19 July by Rev. Exum Everett. p. 201

20 January 1785. MATHEW JONES, b. 18 Mar. 1758, d. 18 July 1838, and MOLLY CRUMPLER. See Rev. Sol. Bur. in Indiana p. 213. Ministers' returns p. 635

21 July 1785. MATHEW JONES and ANN GARDINER. Ministers' returns p. 636

19 January 1774. NATHAN JONES of Surry Co. and LUCY EDWARDS, dau. of Micajah Edwards, deceased. Sur. Benjamin Blunt. Wit. Richard Kello. p. 20

22 December 1797. NATHANIEL JONES and POLLY WOOD, dau. of Sarah Wood. Sur. William Summerell. Wit. Samuel Kello, Jr. Married 25 Dec. by Rev. Drewry Lane. p. 118

11 October 1764. ROBERT JONES and ELIZABETH FITZHUGH. Sur. James Jones. Wit. Richard Kello. p. 10

13 January 1774. ROBERT JONES and PRUDENCE FREEMAN, dau. of Henry Freeman. Sur. Richard Kello. Wit. Arthur Foster, Arthur Freeman and James Jones. p. 20

12 January 1797. ROBERT JONES and MARY PORTER. Sur. John Mundell. Wit. John D. Haussmann. p. 113

28 December 1789. SALTER WILLIAM JONES and REBECCA WRIGHT. Sur. Anselm Jones. Wit. Samuel Kello. p. 64

1 October 1786. THOMAS JONES and SALLY WILKINSON. Married by George Gurley, Rector of St. Luke's Parish, Episcopal Church. Ministers' returns p. 644

31 March 1809. JAMES JORDAN and POLLY IRELAND. Married by Rev. Benjamin Barnes, Methodist. Ministers' returns p. 658

12 June 1794. JOHN JORDAN and REBECCA JONES. Sur. Randolph Rawles. Wit. John D. Haussmann and Jacob Bailey. Married 26 June by Rev. Newit Vick. p. 97

25 December 1785. PERRY JORDAN and BATHSHEBA HARPER, dau. of John Harper. Sur. John Rogers. Wit. Samuel Kello, Hansel Harper and John Harper, Jr. Married 29 Dec. by Rev. John Maglamre. p. 43

9 December 1790. THOMAS JORDAN and PRISCILLA APPLEWHITE. Sur. John Applewhite. p. 69

2 March 1786. PHILIP JOY and SUKEY REECE. Ministers' returns p. 636

8 August 1781. ABSALOM JOYNER and CELIA DRAKE. Sur. Lewis Joyner. Wit. Richard Kello. p. 31

26 June 1790. AMOS JOYNER and MILLEY BRIDGERS. Sur. Lewis Joyner. Wit. Benjamin Drew. p. 66

25 January 1794. BAKER JOYNER and CHRISTIAN WRIGHT, dau. of Sarah Wright. Sur. Absalom Joyner. p. 94

28 January 1794. BRITTAIN JOYNER, JR. and MARY COUNCIL, dau. of Martha Blyth. Sur. Johnson Council. Wit. John Beaton and Richard Kello. p. 95

21 May 1804. ELISHA JOYNER and POLLY WHITNEY. Sur. Joshua Whitney. Wit. Benjamin Cobb. See Elisha Whitney. p. 160

9 March 1786. GILES JOYNER and MILLY SIMMONS. Ministers' returns 4 April 1786. Sur. Richard Vick. p. 45

9 November 1784. JACOB JOYNER and MARTHA POWERS. Ministers' returns p. 635

23 December 1795. JEREMIAH JOYNER, son of Martha Joyner, and Eleanor Tyler. Sur. Charles Council. p. 105

8 September 1791. JOHN JOYNER and MASON HOLT. Sur. John Barnes. Wit. John D. Haussmann. Married 3 Nov. by Rev. George Gurley, Rector of St. Luke's Parish, Episcopal Church. p. 74

8 March 1787. JOSEPH JOYNER and SYLVIA SIMMONS. Sur. William Simmons. p. 51

22 July 1789. JOSEPH JOYNER and POLLY JOYNER. Sur. William Joyner. Married 30 July by Rev. D.C. Barrow. p. 60

18 December 1809. JOSEPH JOYNER and MASON WILLS, dau. of William and Mary Ben Wills. Sur. James Wills. Wit. James Rochelle. p. 196

15 January 1788. JORDAN JOYNER and LYDIA WRIGHT. Sur. Lewis Joyner. Married 31 Jan. by Rev. D.C. Barrow. p. 54

20 September 1786. KINCHEN JOYNER and AGATHY DRAKE. Sur. Joshua Joyner. Wit. Francis Young, Jr. Married 21 Sept. by Rev. David Barrow. p. 47

20 May 1778. LEWIS JOYNER (Joiner) and LUCY WILLIAMS, dau. of Nicholas Williams. Sur. John Davis. Wit. Samuel Kello. p. 26

30 January 1790. LEWIS JOYNER and LYDIA BEALE (Beall), dau. of Richard Beall. Sur. Thomas Love. Wit. Samuel Kello and Francis Young, Jr. p. 64

31 December 1801. LEWIS JOYNER and SALLY LOVE. Sur. Amos Joyner. Wit. Samuel Kello, Jr. p. 149

13 August 1786. MATHEW JOYNER and PATIENCE POPE. Sur. Giles Joyner. Wit. Francis Young, Jr. Married by Rev. George Gurley, Rector of St. Luke's Parish, Episcopal Church. Ministers' returns p. 643

16 January 1809. MATTHEW JOYNER and JANE WILLS, dau. of William and Mary Ben Wills. Sur. Absalom Joyner. Wit. Samuel Kello. p. 188

10 October 1783. MOSES JOYNER and HONOUR BRADSHAW. Married by Rev. David Barrow. Ministers' returns p. 637

22 May 1809. REUBEN JOYNER and ELIZABETH DENNONG, dau. of Polly Hogg. Sur. Benjamin Bradshaw. Wit. Thad. Powell and Samuel Kello. p. 191

24 September 1788. ROBERT JOYNER and CELIA ENGLISH (Selah on back of bond). Sur. Lewis Joyner. Wit. Samuel Kello. Married 30 Sept. by Rev. D.C. Barrow. p. 56

22 January 1787. SIMMONS JOYNER and ANN JOHNSON. Penninah Johnson mother and guardian. Sur. Burwell Bunn. Wit. Francis Young, Jr. Note: Penninah was widow of John Johnson will proved 1783. Married 25 Jan. by Rev. David Barrow. p. 50

22 December 1807. SINKSINE (?) JOYNER and PERMILIA BARNES, dau. of Jacob Barnes. Sur. John Johnston. Wit. William Hart and Benjamin Cobb. p. 181

30 July 1797. WILEY JOYNER (Willis Joiner) and LUCY VICK, dau. of Council Vick who consents. Sur. Thomas Newsum, Jr. Wit. Samuel Kello. Married 3 Aug. by Rev. Benjamin Barnes, Methodist. p. 115

9 November 1768. CHARLES JUDKINS of Sessex Co. and MARTHA WESTBROOKE, dau. of Thomas Westbrooke. Sur. Isham Gilliam of Sussex Co. Wit. Richard Kello. p. 14

17 October 1783. JORDAN JUDKINS and SALLY WARREN. Sally of
Surry Co. Married by Rev. David Barrow. Ministers' returns
p. 637

24 February 1803. RICHARD B. KE_____ and ELIZABETH M. BURGESS.
Married by Rev. Drewry Lane. Ministers' returns p. 653

20 April 1807. NATHANIEL KELLO and PHEREBA ARTIS. Sur. John
Rawles. Wit. Samuel Kello. p. 178

23 August 1778. WILLIAM KELLOW and ELIZABETH RIDLEY TAYLOR.
Sur. Samuel Brown. Wit. Lucy Taylor and John Wright. Note:
She must have been a widow as her dau. Lucy Taylor married
Jesse Wilkinson 11 May 1786. p. 27

14 December 1786. JOHN KELLY (Celley) and MARGARET GLOVER.
Sur. James Doughtry. Wit. Samuel Kello. Married 19 Dec. by
Rev. Geo. Gurley, Rector St. Luke's Parish, Episcopal Church.
p. 49

1 March 1792. GEORGE KEMP (Kem on back of bond) and HANNAH
WRIGHT. Sur. Matthew Kemp. Wit. Willis Woodly and Samuel
Kello. p. 80

11 January 1772. JOHN KERBY and ELIZABETH DRAKE. Sur. Nicholas
Williams. Wit. Samuel Kello. p. 17

30 December 1797. MOODY KERBY and NANCY KAR. Wit. Samuel
Kello. (Consent date) Moody Kirby and Nancy Carr in Ministers'
returns 29 Dec. 1797. There is a bond under date of 10 Dec.
1789 bearing the same names. Married by Rev. Drewry Lane.
p. 118

12 November 1810. MILES KIRSEY and NANCY BASS. Sur. Cordell
Reed. Wit. Joseph Gurley and Samuel Kello. p. 203

13 May 1756. WIGGINS KILLEGREW and HANNAH ALSABROOKE. Sur.
Samuel Alsabrooke. Wit. Richard Kello. p. 3

17 December 1804. WILLIAM KINCHEN (Kitchen) and SALLY DAVIS.
Sur. Richard Pond. Wit. Sally Davis and Benjamin Cobb. Married
27 Dec. by Rev. Drewry Lane. p. 164

25 January 1783. JOHN KINDRED and SALLY DAY. Sur. Benjamin
Kindred. Wit. Samuel Kello. p. 35

25 January 1770. BENJAMIN KIRBY and ANN SIMMONS, dau. of
Charles Simmons, deceased. Sur. William Simmons. Wit. Samuel
Kello. p. 15

12 September 1777. JOHN KIRBY and ANN MEACOM (Mecom). Sur.
Samuel Kello. Wit. James R. Kello. p. 24

10 December 1789. MOODY KIRBY and NANCY CARR. Sur. Barnaby
Drake. Wit. Francis Young, Jr. p. 63

12 January 1775. SILAS KIRBY and DIANAH CALTHORPE. Sur. Edmund Tyler. Wit. Samuel Kello. p. 22

16 January 1787. THOMAS KIRBY and REBECCA BASS, sister of Mecklin Bass. Sur. Miles Kirby. Wit. Samuel Kello. p. 50

17 December 1798. WILLIAM KIRBY and ELIZABETH TURNER, consent of Mildred Turner. Sur. Jesse Holt. Wit. W. Evans. p. 124

7 June 1804. DIXON KITCHEN and PATSY MEDFORD. Married by Rev. Drewry Lane. Ministers' returns p. 653

29 December 1807. ENOS KITCHEN and PEGGY TRAVIS. Sur. John Kitchen. Wit. Benjamin Cobb. p. 181

6 June 1785. ETHELDRED KITCHEN and PATSEY (Patty) HINES. Sur. John Hines. 8 June 1785 in Ministers' returns. p. 40

6 February 1790. JOHN KITCHEN and MARTHA WILLIAMS, dau. of Matthew and Anne Williams. Sur. Cordall Drake. Wit. Francis Young, Jr. and Absalom Joyner. p. 64

31 May 1800. SAMUEL KITCHEN and REBECCA BAILEY. Sur. William Hart. Wit. Samuel Kello. Married 5 June by Rev. William Hargraves. p. 136

28 February 1792. LEWIS KNIGHT and EADY FAUSTER "of age". Sur. Robert Goodwyn. Wit. Willis Woodley and Moby Moore. Foster in minister's returns 1 July. Married by Rev. John Meglamre, Baptist. p. 79

1 January 1805. LEWIS KNIGHT and REBECCA VAUGHAN. Sur. Miles Cary. Wit. Samuel Kello. p. 164

10 September 1795. JOSEPH LAINE (Lain) and MARY DAVIS. Sur. John Davis. Wit. John D. Haussmann. Married 17 Sept. by Rev. Drewry Lane who says Joseph Lane. p. 103

10 July 1788. JAMES LANCASTER and REBECCA WALLIS. Rebecca of Sussex Co. Married by Rev. D.C. Barrow. Ministers' returns p. 641

9 November 1786. CHARLES LAND and MARY COOPER. Sur. Benjamin Butts. Wit. Betty Butts, and Francis Young, Jr. p. 48

4 October 1791. LITTLEBERRY LAND and MARY McLEMERE. Sur. William Ellis. Wit. John D. Haussmann. p. 75

8 February 1787. NATHANIEL LAND and REBECCA HART. Sur. Nicholas Meget, Jr. Married 14 Feb. by Rev. George Gurley, Rector of St. Luke's Parish, Episcopal Church. p. 50

3 March 1792. SAMUEL LANE and ELIZABETH KITCHEN. Sur. Joseph Lane. Wit. John D. Haussmann. Married 8 March by Rev. Drewry Lane. p. 80

17 December 1785. WILLIAM LANE and MARY CHAMPION of Surry Co. Married by Rev. David Barrow. Ministers' returns p. 638

24 December 1799. WILLIAM LANE and LUCY FELTS. Lucy Lane grandmother to Lucy Felts. Sur. Lemuel Hargrave. Wit. Samuel Kello, Jr. and Bobby Lane. Married 26 Dec. by Rev. William Hargrave. p. 131

9 November 1769. THOMAS LANGFORD and ELIZABETH WESTRY (Westra). Sur. Nathan Vasser. Wit. Richard Kello. p. 15

13 July 1788. JOHN LANKFORD and LYDIA BOOLS (?). Married by Rev. D.C. Barrow. Ministers' returns p. 641

21 March 1803. JONATHAN LANKFORD and PATSEY TURNER. Sur. Stephen Lankford. Wit. Benjamin Cobb. p. 153

10 December 1785. STEPHEN LANKFORD and RHODY TURNER. Sur. Joseph Turner. Wit. Francis Young, Jr. Married 15 Dec. by Rev. David Barrow. p. 43

20 February 1809. STEPHEN LANKFORD and ELIZA COUNCIL. Sur. Pettway Johnson. Wit. James Rochelle. p. 189

6 December 1798. ACRILL LAMB and NANCY WASHINGTON. Sur. Harod Brent. Wit. Samuel Kello, Jr. "Acril" in Ministers' returns 20 Dec. Married by Rev. Drewry Lane. p. 123

3 July 1810. WILLIAM LASSITER and REBECCA ADAMS, dau. of Tamer Adams. Sur. John Adams. Wit. Harrison Minton. p. 201

23 August 1787. BENJAMIN LAWRENCE and HONOUR GARDNER. Sur. Jesse Gardner. (Jesse Gainer at top of bond). p. 52

11 February 1791. ELIAS LAWRENCE and RHODA GARDNER. Sur. Henry Gardner. Wit. John D. Haussmann. p. 70

1 July 1762. HARDY LAWRENCE of Isle of Wight Co. and AMEY LORD of Nottoway Parish. Sur. Richard Kello. Wit. Richard Baker and William Drew. p. 7

_____, 1800. HARDY LAWRENCE and _____. Sur. Samuel Corbett. Wit. Samuel Kello, Jr. p. 141

23 May 1794. JACOB LAWRENCE and SALLY WILLIAMS, consent of Joseph Denson (for which one?). Sur. Jesse Crocker. Wit. John D. Haussmann. p. 97

10 January 1793. JOHN LAWRENCE and PHERIBE DARDEN. Sur. Jacob Darden. Wit. John D. Haussmann. p. 87

28 October 1790. WILLIAM LAWRENCE and LIDDA (Lydda) EDWARDS, dau. of William Edwards who is surety. Wit. Thomas Hunt and Samuel Kello. p. 68

20 June 1803. WILLIAM LAWRENCE and WILMOTH B_____. Sur.
Solomon Holmes. p. 155

13 September 1787. JOHN LEE and ABIGAIL CARR (widow). Sur.
Elisha Darden. Wit. Richard Kello. p. 52

21 March 1803. HENRY LENOW and MARTHA SUMMERELL in bond,
Fanny Hugh in consent, dau. of Martha Summerell. Sur. Joseph
Boykin. Wit. Benjamin Cobb. This must be Fanny Hugh or Hough
as Marcha Hough m. Thomas Summerell 19 Aug. 1791. p. 153

23 March 1803. HENRY LENOW and FANNY HOUGH, dau. of Martha
Summerell. Sur. Joseph Boykin. Wit. Benjamin Cobb. p. 153

10 November 1752. BENJAMIN LEWIS and MARY HARRIS, dau. of
Mary Merick. Sur. Timothy Thorp. Wit. Edward Harris and
Richard Kello. p. 1

16 February 1801. ELISHA LEWIS and ELIZABETH JONES. Sur.
Samuel Woodard. Wit. Samuel Kello. p. 143

12 February 1789. EXUM LEWIS and ZILPHA HEDGPETH. Sur. Amos
Council. Wit. Richard Kello. Married 18 Feb. by Rev. D.C.
Barrow. p. 58

22 October 1801. GEORGE LIBERTY and PATIENCE VICK. Sur.
William Pope. Wit. Samuel Kello, Jr. p. 146

22 July 1758. JOHN LITTLE and LUCEY BITTLE, dau. of William
Bittle. Sur. Stephen Williamson. Wit. Richard Kello and Jen.
Hurst. p. 4

2 December 1785. WILLIAM LITTLE and ELIZABETH BASS. p. 42

10 December 1785. WILLIAM LITTLE and MARTHA CRUMPLER. Sur.
John Crumpler. Wit. Samuel Kello. Married by Rev. David
Barrow. Returned 22 Dec. p. 43

10 August 1769. MOSES LOFTIN (Lofting) and SARAH PARKER, dau.
of Drury Parker. Sur. Jeremiah Drew. Wit. Richard Kello. p. 14

19 September 1805. DAVID LONG and ELIZABETH CLANTON. Sur.
River Barker. p. 167

20 October 1806. FREDERICK LONG and REBECCA MOORE, dau. of
Temperance Moore. Sur. Willie Francis. Wit. Samuel Kello and
Thomas Moore. p. 173

29 December 1785. JOHN LONG and POLLY ARMSTRONG. Married by
Rev. John Meglamre. Ministers' returns p. 643

8 September 1774. LITTLEBERRY LONG and ANN SUITER. Sur. John
Suiter (Suter). Wit. Samuel Kello. p. 21

25 September 1786. ELIAS LOVE and MARY DELOACH. Sur. Richard Kello, Jr. Wit. M. Belsches and Francis Young, Jr. p. 47

13 February 1799. WILLIAM LOVE and WILMOTH EXUM. Married by Rev. Drewry Lane. Ministers' returns p. 650

5 April 1808. WILLIAM LOVE and LEVINA EXUM. Sur. Bailey Oberry. Wit. Samuel Kello. p. 184

19 January 1792. LEVI LOWE and SARAH BRITT. Sur. Ledbetter Lowe. Wit. Samuel Kello. p. 87

18 June 1798. JOHN LOWE and CHARLOTTE JOHNSON. Sur. Samuel Barden. p. 121

17 April 1786. JOHN LUCAS and BETSY BLUNT. Ministers' returns p. 637

20 December 1794. BYRD LUNDY and LUCY NICOLSON, dau. of Mary Nicolson. Sur. John Reeves Tiller. Wit. Patsey Lundy and Matilda Nicolson. p. 99

14 July 1804. CAPT. BYRD LUNCY and MARY TURNER, dau. of Thomas Turner. Sur. James Lundy. Married 19 July by Rev. Robert Murrell. p. 161

21 December 1804. JAMES LUNDY and SUSANAH DREWRY. Married by Rev. Robert Murrell. Ministers' returns p. 653

5 January 1805. JAMES LUNDY and SUSAN MYRICK. Sur. Edmund Myrick. Wit. Samuel Kello. Married 8 Jan. by Rev. James M. Kindred. p. 164

29 May 1805. JOHN H. LUNDY and SUSANNA HORTON. Sur. James Brantley. Wit. Robert Mabry, Richard Mabry and Mary Lundy. p. 166

14 January 1796. WILLIAM LUNDY and NANCY MEGLAMRE. Sur. John Meglamre. Wit. John D. Haussmann. Married by Rev. John Meglamre, Baptist. p. 106

10 May 1787. JOHN LUTER and WINEFRED MORRELL. Sur. Philip Davis. Wit. Francis Young, Jr. Married 12 May by Rev. George Gurley, Rector of St. Luke's Parish, Episcopal Church. p. 51

25 November 1793. JOHN LUTER and ALICE DUCK. Sur. Samuel Corbitt. Wit. James Chalmers. p. 92

18 January 1808. MATTHEW LUTER and OLLIFER JOHNSON. Sur. Pettway Johnson. Wit. Benjamin Cobb. p. 182

30 September 1806. THOMAS JONES MABRY and MARY LUNDY. Sur. Newit Harris. p. 173

7 December 1791. JOHN MACKIE and HANNAH DRURY. Sur. Benjamin Broodshaw. Wit. John D. Haussmann. p. 76

11 July 1793. JOEL MACLEMORE (McLemore) and BETSEY THOMAS, dau. of Mary Thomas. Sur. Humphrey Drewry. Wit. John D. Haussmann and Samuel Kello. p. 90

8 May 1787. WILLIAM MACLENY and FRANCES MOUNTFORT, dau. of Sarah Mountfort. Sur. Thomas Mountfort, Jr. Wit. Francis Young, Jr. p. 51

_____ _____. FREDERICK MACLIN. See Frederick McLin. p. 4&5

11 June 1801. JORDAN MAGEE and AVERY JONES. Sur. John Simons. Wit. Samuel Kello. p. 144

30 June 1783. JAMES MAGET and JANET EVERITT. Sur. Simon Everitt. Wit. Samuel Kello, Marget and 3 July in Ministers' returns. p. 36

20 April 1801. NICHOLAS MAGET and MARY JANE CARR. Consent of Absalom Williams. p. 144

13 October 1791. SAMUEL MAGET and PRISCILLA DREW. Sur. Nathaniel Land. Wit. J.D. Haussmann. Married 18 Oct. by Rev. George Gurley, Rector of St. Luke's Parish, Episcopal Church. p. 75

8 December 1785. WILLIAM MAGET and SALLY MURRAY. Murry on Ministers' returns 18 Dec. Sur. John Harwood. Wit. Francis Young, Jr. p. 43

7 March 1803. WILLIAM MAGET and SALLY EVERITT, dau. of Elizabeth Everitt. Sur. Nicholas Everitt. p. 153

10 December 1772. DANIEL MAHONE and AMY CHAPPELL of Nottoway Parish, dau. of Thomas Chappell who is surety. Wit. Samuel Kello, Thomas Chappell, Jr. and William Chappell. Written Malone two places on the bond. p. 19

26 October 1786. BENJAMIN MALONE and ELIZABETH FIGURES. Married by Rev. George Gurley, Rector of St. Luke's Parish, Episcopal Church. Ministers' returns p. 644

_____ _____. DANIEL MALONE. See Daniel Mahone. p. 19

12 March 1786. JAMES MANEY and MARY ROBERTS. Ministers' returns p. 637

9 May 1794. WILLIAM MANN and OLIVE (Olivia) THORP. Sur. Jacob Newsum. Wit. John D. Haussmann, H. Carris, Newit Claud and John Reese. p. 96

28 March 1796. PETER MANNERY and SALLY JUDKINS. Sur. Baalam Hutchings. Wit. John D. Haussmann, Bermerley Hutchings parent of Sally. p. 107

17 May 1787. WILLIAM MANRY and ELIZABETH JOYNER. Married by Rev. David Barrow. Ministers' returns p. 639

20 February 1809. JOSEPH MARKS and NANCY BRIGGS. Sur. Edward Hantey. Wit. Samuel Kello. p. 189

11 October 1787. NATHAN MARKS and SILVIA MECOM. Samuel Mecom guardian of Sylvia. Sur. Joseph Marks. Wit. Samuel Mecom. p. 53

11 November 1790. STEPHEN MARKS and SUSANNA HARRISON. Sur. Nathan Marks. p. 68

20 December 1786. WILLIAM MARKS and REBECCA WOMACK. Sur. Basil Payne. Wit. Richard Kello. Married 1 Jan. 1787 by Rev. John Meglamre. p. 49

28 June 1800. WILLIAM MARKS and POLLY WOMACK. Sur. John Marks. Wit. Samuel Kello. p. 136

18 February 1783. DEMPSEY MARSHALL and CHARLOTTE ELERY. Sur. Timothy Atkinson. Wit. Samuel Kello. p. 36

10 September 1799. DAVID MASON and ELIZABETH CLAUD. Sur. Rivers Reese. p. 128

27 September 1764. JOHN MASON, JR. and JANE THWEAT (widow). Sur. Henry Gee of Sussex. Wit. Richard Kello. p. 9

21 June 1787. JOHN MASON and ELIZABETH JONES. Sur. Randolph Newsum. Wit. Francis Young, Jr., Joseph Kello and Samuel Kello. p. 52

20 January 1783. LITTLEBERRY MASON and REBECCA BLUNT. Sur. William Blunt. p. 35

29 May 1798. LITTLETON MASON and FRANCES I. BYNUM. Sur. Richard Mabry. Wit. W. Lundy. Frances J in ministers' returns 1 June. Married by Rev. Robert Murrell.⁻ p. 120

9 June 1800. SETH MASON and JANE MASON. Sur. John Rives Tillar. Wit. Samuel Kello; Robert Mabry guardian for Jane. Appointed in County Court of Greensville where her estate lies. p. 136

31 October 1808. THOMAS MASON and MARTHA EDMUND. Wit. Harrd. W. Edmunds. Consent only. p. 186

24 June 1784. WILLIAM MASSENBURG and REBECCA RIDLEY. Ministers' returns p. 634

1 September 1782. SAMUEL MATTHEWS and WINIFRED CHITTY. Ministers' returns p. 631

15 November 1806. IRVIN B. MAYS and POLLY PARKER, dau. of Milly Parker. Wit. Judith Parker, consent only. p. 174

22 December 1772. MATTHEW MEACOM and MARY DRURY, dau. of Samuel Drury. Sur. Benjamin Kirby. Wit. Silas Kirby. p. 19

20 November 1783. JOHN MEALHOUSE and MARTHA JOYNER. Married by Rev. David Barrow. Ministers' returns p. 637

14 April 1796. JAMES MECOM (Meacom) and PATIENCE HARRIS. Sur. John Mecom. Wit. Samuel Kello. Married 23 April by Rev. Robert Murrell. p. 108

_____ 1790. JOHN MECOM and SUSANNA BARHAM. Married by Rev. John Meglamre. Ministers' returns p. 647

18 January 1785. SAMUEL MECOM and REBECCA COBB. Sur. Benjamin Exum. Wit. Samuel Kello. p. 39

22 December 1801. ROBERT MERCER and NANCY BAILEY. Valentine Jenkins is guardian of Nancy and is surety. Wit. William Carrel. p. 148

18 October 1785. JOHN FRANCIS MIERS and ELIZABETH MORRIS, dau. of Nicholas Morris. Sur. Peter Bailey. Ministers' returns 20 Oct. p. 42

10 October 1792. JOHN MILES and ELIZABETH TYLER. Sur. John Wright. Wit. John D. Haussmann. p. 85

2 January 1799. BENJAMIN MILLAR and NANCY FORT. Sur. Owen Myrick. p. 124

9 April 1798. ROBERT MILLAR and MILDRED RIDDICK. Sur. James Millar. p. 120

WILLIAM MILLARD. See William Miller. p. 9

24 October 1789. JAMES MILLER and PATTY RIDDICK. Will Hines consents for Patty. Sur. Thomas Blow. Wit. Francis Young, Jr., Etheldred Turner and Howell Hines. Millar in ministers' returns 10 Nov. Married by Rev. George Gurley, Rector of St. Luke's Parish Episcopal Church. p. 62

4 June 1764. WILLIAM MILLER (4 places in bond it's Millard and in his own signature) and SARAH CROCKER. Consent of Robert Fry as to William. Sur. Benjamin Lewis and Robert Fry. Wit. Edward Fisher, Joseph Langley and Samuel Langley. p. 9

13 September 1792. RANDOLPH MILTON and AMY FELTS. Sur. Randolph Newsum. Wit. John D. Haussmann and John Reese, Sr. p. 84

25 November 1790. JOSHUA MINIARD and CATHARINE (Katy) CROCKER.
Sur. Jethro Charles. Wit. Samuel Kello. p. 69

28 August 1754. CARY MITCHELL, of Elizabeth City Co., and
MARTHA KELLO. Sur. William Wager of James City Co. Wit. Richard
Kello. p. 2

13 October 1773. JOHN MITCHELL and SARAH MAGETT (widow). Sur.
Abraham Mitchell. Wit. Philip Davis and John Davis. p. 20

13 June 1781. PHILIP MOODY and MARY BARNES. Sur. Samuel Kello.
Wit. Nicholas Maget. p. 30

1 November 1791. AARON MOORE and CHARLOTTE HARGROVE. Sur.
Chalres Travis. Wit. John D. Haussmann. Married 3 Nov. by
Rev. Drewry Lane, Methodist. p. 75

3 December 1760. JAMES MOORE and CELIA (Selah) WILLIAMS, dau.
of Jonah Williams. Sur. Benjamin Williams. Wit. Richard Kello
and Thomas Moore. p. 6

22 July 1791. JESSE W. MOORE and MARTHA H. WILLS, dau. of
Elizabeth Gray. Sur. Jacob Joyner, Jr. Wit. John D. Haussmann.
p. 74

5 May 1790. JOHN MOORE and TEMPERANCE RAMSAY. Ramsey in
ministers' returns 9 May. Married by Rev. Robert Murrell. p. 65

8 October 1799. JOHN MOORE and CHARLOTTE EDWARDS. Sur. George
Edwards. Wit. Samuel Kello. p. 128

12 January 1807. JOHN MOORE and EDITH WARREN, dau. of Etheldred
Warren. Sur. Reuben Whitfield. Wit. Benjamin Cobb. p. 176

7 December 1799. DANIEL MORRIS (Morriss) and SARAH JOHNSON,
dau. of Harris Johnson. Sur. Silas Lowe. Wit. Samuel Kello.
p. 130

12 December 1782. HENRY MORRIS and PHEBY LUNDY. Ministers'
returns p. 632

15 September 1802. GEORGE MOSELEY and PRESELLA (Priscilla?)
HARRIS. Married by Rev. Robert Murrel. Ministers' returns
p. 652

8 January 1767. HENRY MOUNGER and BETTY HARRIS, dau. of Henry
Harris. Sur. Jethro Mounger. Wit. Edward Fisher, John Pritchett
and Henry Pritchett. p. 12

25 October 1786. THOMAS MOUNTFORT, JR. and MARY CAMP, consent
of Mary Camp. Sur. Jesse Douglas. Wit. Francis Young, Jr.
Married 26 Oct. by Rev. David Barrow. p. 48

3 February 1781. JOHN MUNDELL, JR. and SARAH FRANCES, dau. of
Thomas Frances. Sur. David Hines. Wit. Samuel Kello. Double
wedding - see David Hines. p. 29

17 December 1810. JOHN MUNDELL and ELIZABETH TUNNELL. Sur.
Henry Blunt. Wit. James Rochelle and Michael Harris. p. 204

16 April 1781. RICHARD MURFEE and ELIZABETH TUCKER. Sur.
Samuel Kello. Ministers' returns say Murphey, Jr. p. 30

10 February 1807. SIMON MURFEE and LYDIA BEAL, dau. of Burwell
and Charity Beal. Sur. Wells Murfee. Wit. Samuel Kello. The
name of the surety may be Mills Murfee. p. 177

16 May 1781. RICHARD MURPHRY, JR. and ELIZABETH TUCKER.
Ministers' returns p. 630

12 July 1792. ROBERT MURRELL and REBEKAH WESTBROOK. Sur.
Etheldred Blake. Wit. Samuel Kello and John D. Haussmann.
"Rebecca" in Ministers' returns 12 Aug. Married by Rev. Robert
Murrell. p. 83

1 November 1806. EVANS MYRICK and MARY ANN WALL. Sur. Richard
Mabry. Wit. Richard Kello and James Lundy. Married 6 Nov. by
Rev. Benjamin Barnes, Methodist. p. 173

11 February 1773. JOHN MYRICK and MARTHA EDMUNDS, consent of
Mary Edmunds. Sur. Owen Myrick. p. 19

20 May 1799. JOHN MYRICK and BETSEY TURNER. Sur. Henry Barrow.
Wit. Samuel Kello, Jr. p. 127

19 December 1803. JOHN MYRICK and POLLY BARHAM. Sur. Benjamin
Barham. Bond says John Myrick "of Owen". Married 29 Dec. by
Rev. Robert Murrell. p. 157

1 September 1810. JOHN MYRICK and ELIZABETH NEWSUM, dau. of
Sarah Newsum. Sur. David Newsum. Wit. James Rochelle. p. 202

9 July 1767. OWEN MYRICK and FANNY NICHOLSON, dau. of Sarah
Nicholson, consent of Joshua Nicholson brother of Fanny who is
surety. Wit. William Myrick and Edward Fisher. p. 12

27 October 1801. OWEN MYRICK and DOLLY P. BARHAM, dau. of
Benjamin Taylor Barham. Sur. Howell Harper. Wit. Samuel Kello,
Jr. p. 147

10 May 1805. ROBERT MYRICK and ELIZABETH JONES. Albridgton
Jones guardian of Elizabeth. Sur. Samuel Kello. Wit. Bolton
Pierce. p. 166

16 January 1772. WILLIAM MYRICK of Sussex Co., and LUCY
NEWSUM, an infant orphan dau. of David Newsum, deceased. Sur.
Soloman Deloach. p. 18

12 January 1804. WILLIAM MYRICK and TEMPERANCE FORT. Married
by Rev. Robert Murrell. Ministers' returns p. 652

16 October 1797. CHARLES McCLEMORE (McLemore) and LUCY ROWE, dau. of John Rowe. Sur. Elijah Johnson. Wit. Samuel Kello, Jr. and J. O. Cick. p. 116

21 June 1787. WILLIAM McCLENNY and FRANCES MOUNTFORT. Married by Rev. David Barrow. Ministers' returns p. 639

30 November 1793. ROBERT McGEE and NANCY POND. Sur. William Pond. Wit. Samuel Kello. p. 92

28 February 1786. HOWEL McLAMORE and LUCY HARRIS. Married by Rev. John Maglamre. Ministers' returns p. 643

19 May 1800. GILLIAM McLEMORE (Gillam Mackelemore) and ANN MARKS. Sur. Nathan Marks. p. 135

13 March 1794. JOHN McLEMORE and SYLVIA REESE. Sur. John Reese. Wit. Samuel Kello. p. 96

22 October 1786. JOHN McLENY (McLency) and MILDRED MOUNTFORT, dau. of Joseph Mountfort. Sur. Thomas Mountfort. Married 23 Nov. by Rev. David Barrow who says McClenney. p. 48

12 October 1758. FREDERICK McLIN (Maclin) and PRISCILLA CLEMENTS, dau. of Benjamin Clements. Sur. Benjamin Clements, Jr. Wit. Richard Kello and Thomas Clements. p. 4

12 June 1760. FREDERICK McLIN (Maclin) and LUCY RAWLINGS. Sur. Peter Butts. p. 5

26 September 1782. ANDREW McMIAL and MOURNING VICK. Ministers' returns p. 631   See Andrew McNeal

13 June 1793. ANDREW McMIAL (McMials) and MARY NEWTON. Sur. John Kindred. Wit. John D. Haussmann and Samuel Kello. p. 90

2 September 1783. JACOB McMIAL and MARY RAYE. Ministers' returns p. 633

14 September 1782. ANDREW McNEAL and MOURNING VICK, dau. of Simon Vick. Sur. Jonas Bryant. Wit. Samuel Kello, Jacob Vick and Jesse Vick. p. 33   See Andrew McMial

25 February 1791. ALEXANDER McNIEL and ANN BENNETT. Sur. Miles Cary. Wit. John D. Haussmann. p. 71

9 May 1794. WILLIAM NANCE and OLIVE THORPE. Sur. Jacob Newsum. Wit. J.D. Haussmann, H. Carris, John Reece and Newit Claude. Ministers' returns p. 96

22 June 1795. WILLIAM NANCE and ELIZABETH ELLIS. Sur. Norento
Ellis. Wit. John D. Haussmann and James B. Womack. Ministers'
returns 23 June. Married by Rev. Robert Murrell. p. 102

12 November 1796. WILLIAM NANCE and POLLY BASS. Sur. William
Claud. Wit. John D. Haussmann and Tho. Powell. p. 110

27 July 1788. EZEKIEL NEIMS of Nansemond Co., and ELIZABETH
BRITT of Isle of Wight Co. Married by Rev. D.C. Barrow.
Ministers' returns p. 641

23 May 1792. THOMAS NEIMS and RHODA HATFIELD. Henry Jones
guardian of Rhoda. Sur. Micajah Griffin. Wit. Willis Woodley
and Samuel Kello. p. 83

10 February 1800. WILLIS NELMS, on face of bond - Knelms on
back of bond, and LUCY BROWNING. Sur. William Hart. Wit.
Samuel Kello, Jr. Married 18 Feb. by Rev. William Hargrave.
p. 133

17 January 1801. GABRIEL NELSON and POLLY TURNER. Sur. Jarrett
Westbrooke. Wit. Edmund Turner, Samuel Wallace, Samuel Kello,
Jr. Married 25 Jan. p. 141

14 April 1792. PETER NEWBY and NANNY CHARITY. Sur. Ned Cornwell
Wit. John D. Haussmann. Married 15 April by Rev. Drewry Lane.
p. 82

4 January 1786. JOHN NEWSOM and CHARLOTTE POPE. Ministers'
returns p. 636

29 May 1764. ROBERT NEWSOM, JR. (Newsum) and MILLEY VICK, dau.
of William and Ann Vick. Robert son of Robert and Elizabeth
Newsom. Sur. Joseph Newsom. Wit. Edward Fisher. p. 9

19 April 1789. WILLIAM NEWSOME and MARY COCKE SIMMONS, dau.
of John Simmons, Sr. Sur. Soloman Delouch. Wit. Samuel Kello.
p. 59

11 February 1804. DAVID NEWSON and POLLY NEWSOM. Sur. Nathaniel
Newsom. Wit. Benjamin Pierce. Married 23 Feb. by Rev. Benjamin
Barnes, Methodist, who says Newsum. p. 158

12 June 1760. JOSEPH NEWSON (Newsum) and PATIENCE JONES (widow).
Sur. Joseph Cobb. p. 5

19 May 1808. CORDALL NEWSUM and SARAH TABOR. Sur. Joel Tabor.
Wit. Samuel Kello. p. 185

28 December 1761. FRANCIS NEWSUM, of Dinwiddie Co., and MARY
SIMMONS, dau. of Benjamin Simmons. Sur. Richard Kello. Wit.
Benjamin Simmons. p. 6

9 January 1782. ISHAM NEWSUM and SALLY NEWSUM, dau. of Patience
Newsum. Sur. Moses Foster. Wit. William Thomas. Note: Joseph
Newsom married 12 June 1760 Patience Jones, widow. Joseph
Newsom's will 16 March 1766 mentions wife Patience and dau.
Sally. p. 32

26 April 1805. JAMES NEWSUM and NANCY BARNES. Sur. Matthew
Murfee. Wit. Bolton Pierce. p. 166

12 April 1800. JOHN NEWSUM and PATSY JOYNER. Sur. John Newsum,
Sr. Wit. Samuel Kello and Council Vick. Married 18 April by
Rev. Benjamin Barnes, Methodist. p. 135

-- February 1803. THOMAS NEWSUM and ELIZABETH VICK. Sur.
Howell Beal. Wit. Benjamin Cobb. Married 6 Mar. by Rev.
Benjamin Barnes, Methodist. p. 153

22 June 1796. TURNER NEWSUM and SILVIAH MURPHEE (Murfee).
Sur. William Turner. Wit. Samuel Kello. Turner Newsom and
Silviah Murfee on Ministers' returns 25 June. Married by Rev.
Robert Murrell. p. 108

13 September 1757. WILLIAM NEWSUM of Dinwiddie Co., and
ELIZABETH GRAY, dau. of J. Gray. Sur. James Wall of Brunswick
Co. Wit. Richard Kello. p. 3

19 January 1802. WILLIAM NEWSUM and NANCY NEWSUM, dau. of Joel
Newson. Sur. William Evans. Wit. Samuel Kello. p. 149

16 June 1800. CHARLES NEWTON and LUCY MORGAN. Sur. Francis
Sterling. Wit. Joel McLemore. p. 136

10 April 1794. HOSEA NEWTON and CRISSY BLAKE. Sur. David
Pope. Wit. John D. Haussmann. p. 96

20 July 1800. WIGGANS (Wiggan) NEWTON and SALLY MORGAN. Sur.
Joel McLemore. Wit. Thomas Willeford. p. 137

8 July 1790. WILLIAM NEWTON and PHEBE WORRELL. Sur. Amos
Worrell. Wit. Francis Young, Jr. p. 66

14 January 1783. EDWARD NIBLET and SALLY HOUGH. John Clayton
guardian of Sally. Sur. John Clayton, Jr. Wit. Samuel Kello.
p. 35

10 December 1795. CHASMON NICHOLSON and MARTHA JONES. Sur.
John Gilliam. Wit. John D. Haussmann. Married by Rev. John
Meglamre, Baptist who says Cheasman. p. 104

26 November 1798. ETHELDRED NICHOLSON and SUSAN NICHOLSON, dau.
of Mark Nicholson. Wit. Zebulon Lewis. Wit. Samuel Kello.
p. 123

10 November 1774. HARRIS NICHOLSON of Sussex Co., and POLLY
EDMUNDS of St. Luke's Parish. Sur. Benjamin Blunt. Wit.
Richard Kello. p. 22

21 April 1803. HOWEL NICH(OLS)ON and SALLY BRIGGS. Married by
Rev. Drewry Lane. Ministers' returns p. 653

4 November 1776. JOHN NICHOLSON and LUCY EDMUNDS. Sur. Thomas
Edmunds. Wit. Harris Nicholson and Sarah Edmunds. p. 23

13 November 1806. JOHN NICHOLSON and EMILY NICHOLSON. Married
by Rev. Drewry Lane. Ministers' returns p. 654

4 March 1808. JOHN NICHOLSON and EDITH RIVERS, dau. of Nancy
Rivers. Sur. William Blow. Wit. Charles B. Nicholson and
Benjamin Cobb. p. 183

8 October 1764. JOSHUA NICHOLSON (Nicolson) and MARY KIRBY JR.,
dau. of William Kirby who is surety. Wit. Richard Kello. p. 10

28 February 1794. ROBERT NICHOLSON and POLLY BUTTS, dau. of
Benjamin Butts. Sur. William Simmons. Wit. Richard Kello and
Samuel Kello. Married 6 March by Rev. John Meglamre, Baptist.
p. 96

25 July 1804. STITH NICHOLSON and ANN M. STEWART, consent only.
p. 161

12 March 1808. AARON NORFLEET and MERIAN ARTIS. Sur. Barnes
Bolling. Wit. Benjamin Cobb. p. 183

2 July 1771. CORDALL NORFLEET and MARY WILKINSON, dau. of
John Wilkinson. Sur. John Powell. Wit. James Williamson and
Richard Kello. p. 16

15 December 1806. JOHN NORRIS and MARTHA LANE. Sur. Edwin
Morris. Wit. Samuel Kello and Mary H. Travis. Married 25
Dec. by Rev. Drewry Lane. p. 175

29 February 1796. JOHN NORSWORTHY and MARY HALVIN (Helvin).
Sur. John Lain. Wit. Samuel Kello. p. 107

24 September 1784. JOSEPH NORSWORTHY and JOANNA HOLT. Ministers' returns p. 635

5 December 1797. THOMAS NORTHROP (Northeross) and HATTY
McGLEMERY (Meglamre). Sur. John Meglamre. Wit. Samuel Kello.
p. 117

16 November 1803. BRIGGS NORVELL and JANE S. MABRY. Sur.
Richard Mabry. Wit. John Peters and James Lundy. p. 157

31 October 1800. BAILEY OBERRY and MARTHA PITMAN. Sur. John
Pitman. Wit. Samuel Kello, Jr. p. 138

21 June 1790. THOMAS OBERRY and PEGGY SPIVEY of Nottoway Parish. Sur. William Spivey. Wit. Mary Spiva. p. 66

20 April 1793. BENJAMIN ODONNILLY and LUCY JOHNSON. Sur. John Odonnilly. Wit. John D. Haussmann. p. 89

26 August 1796. JOHN ODONNILLY and SALLY JOINER. Sur. Benjamin Odonnilly. Wit. Samuel Kello. p. 109

5 February 1782. JOSHUA OLDNER and SALLY FORT, dau. of John Fort. Sur. John Foster. Wit. Samuel Kello and Capt. Samuel Callow. p. 32

5 November 1783. MALACHY (Malachi) OLDNER and MARY FORT. Sur. Robert Fort. Wit. Samuel Kello. p. 37

17 May 1756. BENJAMIN ONEY and BARBARA WELLENS. Sur. William Exum. Wit. Thomas Blunt. p. 3

5 December 1796. BENJAMIN ONEY and ANNE DENSON. Sur. Thomas Hart. Wit. Richard Kello. p. 104

22 June 1793. JOHN ONEY and MARTHA ATKINSON, dau. of John Atkinson. Sur. Samuel Atkinson. Wit. William Atkinson and Samuel Kello. p. 90

20 December 1788. WILLIAM OUTLAND and REBECCA STRINGFIELD, both of Isle of Wight Co. Married by Rev. D.C. Barrow. Ministers' returns p. 641

26 December 1782. ROBERT OWENS and MARSILLA WILLIAMS. Ministers' returns p. 632

14 May 1791. WALTER PAINE (Payne) and SARAH NEWSUM, consent of Basill Payne. Sarah dau. of Francis Newsum who is surety. Wit. Will Hines, John James and Samuel Kello. Married 15 May by Rev. Robert Murrell. p. 73

18 October 1802. EDWARD PARKER and ELIZABETH WILLIAMS. Sur. Jacob Darden. p. 151

15 March 1765. FRANCIS PARKER of Edgecomb Co., N.C., and MARY WILLIAMS, dau. of Nicholas Williams. Sur. Benjamin Williams. Wit. Richard Kello and Martha Williams. p. 10

15 April 1799. HENRY PARKER and REBECCA FITZHUGH. Sur. James Drew. Wit. Samuel Kello, Jr. p. 126

12 February 1789. IVEY (Ivy) PARKER and PENNY GARNER. Sur. Jesse Garner. Married 19 Feb. by Rev. D.C. Barrow. p. 58

20 December 1804. JESSE PARKER and SALLY WILLIAMS. Married by Rev. Benjamin Barnes, Methodist. Ministers' returns p. 657

23 October 1767. RICHARD PARKER and MARY BLUNT. Sur. Richard
Kello. Wit. Edward Fisher, Thomas Blunt and Ann Blunt. p. 12

21 April 1766. THOMAS PARKER and JANE RIDLEY, dau. of James
Ridley. This is consent only. p. 11

1 March 1787. WILLIAM PARKER and MARTHA BREWER. Married by
Rev. David Barrow. Ministers' returns p. 639

4 April 1801. WILLIAM PARKER and SALLY WINBORNE. Sur. Daniel
Boykin. p. 143

3 February 1803. JOHN PARNOL and POLLY STEPHENSON. Sur.
Jordan Stephenson. Wit. Samuel Kello. p. 152

18 March 1796. WILLIAM PARRISH and ANN SIMMONS. Sur. James
Bennett. Wit. John D. Haussmann. p. 107

19 September 1805. SOLOMON W. PASTEUR and PATSY MOSS BOYKIN,
consent of Joel Boykin. Sur. David Boykin. Wit. Bolton Pierce.
p. 167

17 December 1798. DREWRY PATE and BETSY THORPE. Randal Reese
her guardian. Sur. Jordan Pate. Wit. John Reese. p. 124

26 January 1795. HERBERT (Harbert) PATE and CHARLOTTE ADAMS.
Sur. John Pate. Wit. James Chalmers. Married 5 Feb. by Rev.
Robert Murrell. p. 100

14 May 1795. JORDAN PATE and ELIZABETH ADAMS. Sur. William
Pate. Wit. John D. Haussmann. Married 3 June by Rev. Robert
Murrell. p. 101

9 December 1790. THOMAS PATE and LUCY ADAMS "of age". Sur.
Peterson Ivey. p. 69

26 September 1783. WILLIAM PATE and REBECCA HAIL. Ministers'
returns p. 633

27 January 1791. THOMAS PAYNE (Paine) and AGNES ANDREWS. Sur.
Thomas Clements Butts. Wit. John D. Haussmann. Married 3 Feb.
by Rev. Robert Murrell. p. 70

24 February 1799. DEMPSEY PEALE and JUDITH BAKER SEAY. Sur.
Benjamin Barnes. Wit. Samuel Kello. Married by Rev. Benjamin
Barnes, Methodist. p. 125

3 December 1800. HENRY PEBWORTH and ELIZABETH BOYD. Sur.
David Edwards. Wit. Samuel Kello, Jr. p. 139

5 April 1789. JOHN PEBWORTH and EDY SAVAGE. Married by Rev.
D.C. Barrow. Ministers' returns p. 642

20 August 1800. WILLIAM PEBWORTH and POLLY GLOVER. Sur. William Washington. Wit. John Cobb. p. 137

31 August 1784. WILLIAM PEDIN and REBECCA DORMAN. Ministers' returns p. 635

23 May 1792. BENJAMIN PEETE and ANN BLUNT, dau. of Benjamin Blunt. Sur. Archibald Parker. Wit. Willis Woodley. p. 83

22 August 1764. THOMAS PEETE of Brunswick Co., and JUDITH CLEMENTS of Nottoway Parish, dau. of Benjamin Clements. Sur. Richard Kello. Wit. Will Urquhart, Thomas Clements and Benjamin Clements, Jr. p. 9

18 April 1778. THOMAS PEETE of Sussex Co., and MARY JONES (widow). Sur. Richard Kello. p. 26

30 September 1772. PETER BELHAM, JR. of Brunswick Co., and PARTHENIA BROWN, consent of John Atkinson. Sur. Augustine Willis. Wit. James Balfour. p. 18

8 June 1780. JAMES PENNINGTON and RACHAEL VICK, dau. of William Vick. Sur. Burwell _____. p. 29

31 October 1797. ANTHONY PERSONS (Person) and ELIZABETH BROWNE (Brown). Sur. Jeremiah Drake. Wit. Samuel Kello and Albridgeton Brown. p. 116

12 May 1768. BENJAMIN PERSON of Bute Co., North Carolina, and LUCRETIA BROWNE, dau. of Jesse Browne. Sur. Richard Kello. Wit. Edward Fisher. p. 13

10 March 1768. JOHN PERSON and MARY HOWELL. Sur. William Person. Wit. Edward Fisher and Hartwell Howell. p. 13

26 January 1772. PHILIP PERSON and TEMPERANCE THORPE. Sur. Peterson Thorpe. Wit. Richard Kello. p. 18

17 January 1801. TURNER PERSON and POLLY HARRISON. Sur. William Harrison. Wit. Samuel Kello. Married 29 Jan. p. 141

10 November 1757. WILLIAM PERSON and MARY THORPE. Sur. Timothy Thorpe. p. 3

15 December 1762. BATT PETERSON of Brunswick Co., and MARY TAYLOR. William Taylor brother and guardian of Mary. Sur. Henry Taylor. Wit. Richard Kello, Francis Hamlin and Thomas Moss. p. 7

28 December 1807. JACQUELEN PETERSON and ELZA (?) TAYLOR. Sur. William Taylor. Wit. Benjamin Cobb. p. 181

29 January 1804. PETER PETERSON and ELIZABETH NEWSOM. Married by Rev. Robert Murrell. Ministers' returns p. 652

7 April 1765. WILLIAM PETERSON and SALLY WILLIAMSON, dau. of Benjamin Williamson. Sur. Lewis Williamson. Wit. Richard Kello and John Wilkenson. p. 10

3 January 1787. FRANCIS PHILLIPS and FANNY BARHAM. Married 30 Jan. by Rev. John Maglamre. p. 49

17 January 1801. HENRY PHILLIPS and CRECY HARRISON. Sur. William Harrison. Wit. Samuel Kello. p. 141

10 October 1797. JOHN PHILLIPS and MARY BRYANT (Tempy on consent). Sur. William Bryant, father of Tempy. Wit. Samuel Kello, Jr. and Catey Taylor. p. 115

22 October 1797. JOHN PHILLIPS and TEMPERANCE PORTER. Married by Rev. Benjamin Barnes, Methodist. Ministers' returns p. 648

19 January 1750. JOSEPH PHILIPS and SARAH EXUM, spinster. Sur. Benjamin Exum. Wit. Richard Kello. 1751 on back of bond. p. 1

23 February 1804. WILLIAM PHILIPS and SALLY ELLERY. Married by Rev. Robert Murrell. Ministers' returns p. 652

3 August 1801. NATHANIEL PIERCE and PRISCILLA RIDDICK. Sur. Jesse Battle. Wit. Samuel Kello, Jr. p. 145

25 June 1809. RICE B. PIERCE and FANNY COOK, dau. of Elizabeth Cook. Sur. Harrison Minton. Married by Rev. Benjamin Barnes, Methodist. p. 192

19 September 1793. SPENCER PIERCE and MARY CALVERT. Sur. Samuel Calvert. Wit. John D. Haussmann. p. 91

21 September 1809. SPENCER PIERCE and EMELY BRIGGS. Married by Rev. Benjamin Barnes, Methodist. Ministers' returns p. 659

24 February 1800. JOHN PITMAN and NANCY SALTER. Sur. William Wellons. Wit. Samuel Kello, Jr. p. 134

18 December 1793. PHILIP PITMAN and DIANAH CLARKE. Sur. John D. Haussmann. Wit. Richard Kello. p. 92

26 June 1766. WALTER PITT of North Carolina and MARTHA WILLIAMS, dau. of Nicholas Williams. Sur. John Williams of North Carolina. Wit. Richard Kello, Ann Williams and Elizabeth Williams. p. 11

12 February 1798. BEAUFORD PLEASANT of Sussex Co., and REBECCA CORRELL, consent of Jessey Corrall. Sur. Jesse Brittle. Wit. Samuel Kello. Married 17 Feb. by Rev. Drewry Lane. p. 119

6 January 1784. BURWELL PLEASANTS and MARY POND. Ministers'
returns p. 634

13 September 1810. CALTHORPE POND and NANCY VICK, dau. of J.
Vick. Sur. Jesse Vick. Wit. Samuel Kello. Married by Rev.
Drewry Lane. p. 202

8 August 1803. DANIEL POND and POLLY WOOD, dau. of MARY WOOD.
Sur. Thomas Wood. Wit. Bolton Pierce. p. 155

25 September 1792. DREWRY (Drury) POND and TABYTHA JOHNSON.
Sur. Shadrach Johnson. Wit. Samuel Kello. p. 84

29 April 1782. JOHN HAWKINS POND and ELEANOR CLIFTON CALTHORPE.
Sur. Samuel Kello. Wit. Edmund Tyler. p. 32

18 July 1793. JOHN POND, JR., and MARY DRURY. Sur. John
Pond, Sr. Wit. John D. Haussmann, Samuel Kello. p. 90

17 December 1806. JOSEPH POND and MARY SIMMONS. Married by
Rev. Drewry Lane. Ministers' returns p. 654

15 June 1801. LEMUEL POND and NANCY LUNDY. Sur. Samuel Kitchen.
Wit. Samuel Kello, Jr. p. 145

20 April 1807. PETER POND and ANNA WELLONS. Sur. John H. Pond.
Wit. Samuel Kello. Married 23 April by Rev. Drewry Lane.
p. 178

1 September 1783. RICHARD POND, JR., and ELIZABETH HEATH. Sur.
Samuel Kello. p. 37

28 March 1805. RICHARD POND and PATSEY POND. Ministers' returns
p. 654

9 May 1773. SAMUEL POND and MARTHA KIRBY, dau. of Richard
Kirby. Sur. Benjamin Kirby. Wit. Samuel Kello, John Sanders
and Silas Kirby. p. 20

20 February 1804. SAMUEL POND and ANN JOYNER. Sur. Amos
Gardner. Wit. Bolton Pierce. p. 159

26 May 1808. SAMUEL POND and DISCA HOLDING. Sur. Daniel Pond.
p. 185

24 January 1789. THOMAS POND and MASON COTTON. Sur. Herbert
Cotton. Married 26 Jan. by Rev. D.C. Barrow. p. 58

19 August 1799. AUGUSTINE POPE and POLLY WORRELL. Sur. James
Worrell. Wit. Benjamin Worrell. Married 22 Aug. by Rev.
Benjamin Barnes, Methodist. p. 128

9 April 1795. DAVID POPE (on face of bond - NATHAN POPE on back of bond) and NANCY JOHNSON. Sur. John Johnson. p. 101

24 March 1796. EDWIN POPE and PATSEY SCARBROUGH. Sur. Will Pope. Wit. Richard Kello, Nathan Pope and Elisha Williams. p. 107

30 January 1787. EVANS POPE and SARAH BARNES, dau. of Jacob and Elizabeth Barnes. Sur. Benjamin Barnes. Wit. Francis Young, Jr. Married 6 Feb. by Rev. George Gurley, Rector of St. Luke's Parish, Episcopal Church. p. 50

19 March 1798. HARDY POPE and SALLY WESTRAY. Jeremiah Westray guardian of Sally. Sur. Jesse Bracy. Wit. Polly Bracy, John Lowe and Samuel Kello, Jr. p. 120

21 April 1785. HENRY POPE and PATTY LAWRENCE. Ministers' returns p. 635

23 November 1794. HENSON POPE and NANCY WORRELL, dau. of Benjamin Worrell. Sur. Nathaniel Pope. Wit. Samuel Kello. p. 98

8 December 1796. HOWEL POPE and SALLY POPE. Certificate of marriage 22 Dec. 1796 by Rev. Benjamin Barnes. p. 111

16 December 1799. JESSE POPE and SALLY CRUMPLER. Sur. William Crumpler. Wit. Samuel Kello. p. 130

15 December 1800. JESSE POPE (top, bottom and back of bond) and NANCY STOREY. Sur. Benjamin Johnston. Wit. Samuel Kello, Jr. Married 18 Dec. by Rev. Benjamin Barnes, Methodist. See Jesse Story. p. 140

10 April 1784. JOEL POPE and SALLY GARRIS. Married by Rev. David Barrow. Ministers' returns p. 638

8 August 1765. JOHN POPE and ANN UNDERWOOD. Sur. Edmund Day. p. 10

23 December 1786. JOHN POPE and FANNY EVANS. Married by Rev. George Gurley, Rector of St. Luke's Parish, Episcopal Church. Ministers' returns p. 644

10 October 1793. JOHN POPE and PRISCILLA HARGRAVE. Sur. John Claud. Wit. John D. Haussmann. p. 91

21 December 1793. JOHN POPE and ELIZABETH JOHNSON. Sur. Britain Barnes. Wit. John D. Haussmann. p. 93

19 January 1794. JOHN POPE and MASON BRADSHAW (Mary Bradshaw on back of bond). Sur. Hardy Pope. Wit. Samuel Kello. p. 94

12 March 1805. JOHN POPE and SALLY EDMUNDS. Sur. William Saunders. Wit. Bolton Pierce and Samuel Kello. p. 165

9 January 1801. JONAS (Jones) POPE and ELIZABETH JONES. Sur.
Jesse Pope. Wit. Nathan Pope, Samuel Kello, Jr. Ministers'
returns 13 Jan. say Jones Pope. p. 141

14 June 1793. JOSIAH POPE and RHODA DRAKE. Sur. Reuben Pope.
Wit. John D. Haussmann. p. 90

10 October 1795. JOSIAH POPE and PRISCILLA MATTHEWS. Sur.
Jacob Barrett. Wit. Samuel Kello. Married 15 Oct. by Rev.
Newit Vick. p. 103

4 February 1801. KETON POPE and MARTHA WOODARD, dau. of S.
Woodard. Sur. John Woodard. Married 12 Feb. Ministers' returns
say Katen Pope. p. 143

18 December 1809. KINCHEN POPE and EDITH SPENCER. Sur. John
Spencer. Married 26 Dec. by Rev. Benjamin Barnes, Methodist.
p. 196

9 October 1783. NATHAN POPE and POLLY POPE (on face of bond,
Sally on back of bond.) Sur. Joseph Norsworthy. Polly in
Ministers' returns. p. 37

22 December 1794. NATHAN POPE and SALLY VICK (Salah). Sur.
Samuel Woodard. Wit. Samuel Kello. p. 99

9 April 1795. NATHAN POPE and NANCY JOHNSON. Sur. John
Johnson. See David Pope. p. 101

29 October 1806. NATHAN POPE and REBECCA JOYNER. Married by
Rev. Benjamin Barnes, Methodist. Ministers' returns p. 657

22 January 1791. RICHARD POPE and MARY BESTS (on face of
bond - Mary Betts on back of bond), dau. of Sarah Butts (in
consent). Sur. Jethro Charles. Wit. Benjamin Owen. p. 70

9 January 1795. SAMPSON POPE and NANCY LAWRENCE. Sur. John
Carr. Wit. John D. Haussmann. Married 29 Jan. by Rev.
Benjamin Barnes, Methodist. p. 100

3 February 1778. SIMON POPE and ANN POPE, both of St. Luke's
Parish. Sur. Robert Newsum. Wit. Samuel Kello. p. 25

31 July 1783. THOMAS POPE and ELIZABETH UNDERWOOD. Ministers'
returns p. 633

16 February 1784. THOMAS POPE and MARY GRESSWITT or Greswith.
Ministers' returns p. 634

15 March 1809. THOMAS POPE and POLLY SCARBOROUGH. Sur.
Nathan Pope. Wit. James Rochelle and Edwin Pope. Married 17
Mar. by Rev. Benjamin Barnes, Methodist. p. 190

12 December 1786. WILLIAM POPE (JOHN POPE in Ministers' returns 23 Dec. 1786), and FANNY EVANS. Sur. Henry Oberry. Wit. Samuel Kello. p. 49

3 December 1792. WILLIAM POPE, son of John Pope who is surety, and MARY FRANCIS, dau. of William Francis. Wit. John D. Haussmann and Samuel Kello. p. 86

2 December 1803. GIDEON PORCH and JEEN HARRISON. Married by Rev. Robert Murrell. See Gideon Portis. Ministers' returns p. 652

25 December 1785. DANIEL PORTER and ELIZABETH MUNDALL, dau. of John Mundall. Sur. Jacob Porter. Wit. Richard Kello. p. 43

19 January 1801. DREWRY (Drury) PORTER and TABITHA PORTER, both of Nottoway Parish. Sur. Jacob Porter. Wit. Noel Vick. Married 21 Jan. p. 142

18 March 1793. HENRY PORTER and MARTHA JOINER (Joyner). Sur. John Woodard. Wit. Samuel Kello. p. 88

27 March 1795. JAMES PORTER and DELILAH UNDERWOOD. Sur. John Underwood. Wit. Richard Kello and Samuel Kello. p. 101

28 February 1791. NATHAN PORTER and ELIZABETH TURNER, dau. of Jacob Turner. Sur. Thomas Porter. Wit. John D. Haussmann. Married 22 March by Rev. Robert Murrell. p. 71

29 December 1789. THOMAS PORTER and LUCY NEWSUM, dau. of Jacob Newsum. Sur. Elias Atkinson. Wit. Samuel Kello. Married 31 Dec. by Rev. George Gurley, Rector of St. Luke's Parish, Episcopal Church. p. 64

28 October 1790. THOMAS PORTER and CHARLOTTE UNDERWOOD, dau. of Matthew and Charlotte Underwood. Sur. Nathan Porter. Wit. Francis Young, Jr. p. 68

28 October 1803. GIDEON PORTIS and JANE HARRISON. Sur. Alfred Howell. Wit. Solomon Harrison, Thomas Harrison. See Gideon Porch. p. 156

18 September 1783. KIRBY PORTEUS and MARY WINDHAM. Ministers' returns p. 633

23 July 1800. ARTIS POWELL and LEVINIA (Viney) ARTIS (Artist). Absalam Artist consents for Viney. Sur. Hanson Pope. Wit. Samuel Kello. Married 18 Aug. by Rev. Benjamin Barnes. p. 137

13 August 1789. DREW POWELL and SOPHIA POWELL, dau. of John Powell. Sur. Michael Warren. Wit. Francis Young, Jr. p. 61

8 September 1791. JOHN POWELL and REBECCA JAMES. Sur. John Barrow. Wit. John D. Haussmann. Married 10 Sept. by Rev. Robert Murrell. p. 75

23 July 1797. WILLIAM POWELL and BEEDY HUSK. Married by Rev. Benjamin Barnes, Methodist. Ministers' returns p. 648

28 December 1791. JOHN PRESSON and AVARILLA HARRIS, dau. of Harmon Harris. Sur. Randolph Harris. Wit. John D. Haussmann. p. 77

18 April 1788. SAMUEL PRETLOW and ANN CRICHLOW. Sur. William Bailey. p. 55

8 May 1810. THOMAS PRETLOW, JR. and JANE W. DENSON. Sur. George Bailey. Wit. Samuel Pretlow, Henry Sikes and Harrison Minton. p. 200

20 June 1808. JOHN PRINCE and ELIZABETH FORT. Sur. Lewis Fort. Wit. Samuel Kello. p. 185

21 January 1809. PETER PURSELL and SALLY SUMMERELL. Sur. Benjamin Crumpler. Wit. James Rochelle and Samuel Kello. p. 188

23 December 1798. PHILIP RAIFORD (Rayford) and MILLE JOHNSON. Sur. William Raiford (Rayford). Wit. Samuel Kello. p. 124

25 December 1803. WILLIAM RAILEY and ALSEY BRYANT. Married by Rev. Benjamin Barnes, Methodist. See William Bailey. Ministers' returns p. 656

8 January 1784. ANANIAS RANDALL and TEMPERANCE PERSON. Sur. Joshua Thorp. p. 38

27 June 1789. JOHN RAWLES and TABITHA BARRETT, dau. of Edmond and Genet Barrott. Sur. Josiah West Cathon. Married 2 July by Rev. D.C. Barrow. p. 60

23 December 1794. RANDOLPH RAWLES and RHODA WORRELL. Sur. John Rawles. Wit. John D. Haussmann. Married 25 Dec. by Rev. Newit Vick. p. 99

1 June 1808. ROBERT RAWLINGS and LYDIA BRADSHAW. Sur. Jacob Bradshaw. Wit. James Rochelle and Benjamin Cobb. p. 185

March 1796. JOHN RAY and SALLY JACOBS. Sur. James Hill. Wit. Samuel Kello. p. 107

16 December 1793. ROBERT RAY and HANNAH DAVIS. Sur. Henry Davis. Wit. John D. Haussmann. See Robert Wren. p. 92

16 September 1799. WILLIAM RAY and MERIAM JACOB. Sur. Elisah Atkinson. Wit. Samuel Kello, Jr. Meriam Jacobs in Ministers' returns 29 Sept. Married by Rev. Benjamin Barnes, Methodist. p. 128

5 January 1793. WILLIAM RAYFORD and MILLEY SUMMERELL. Sur.
Boaz Guin Summerell. Wit. John D. Haussmann. p. 86

14 April 1796. ETHELDRED RAYLEIGH and SALLY HOLT. Sur. Benjamin
Rayleigh. Wit. Samuel Kello and John D. Haussmann. p. 108

19 November 1798. CORDALL REED and DELILAH HERSEY. Sur. James
Sweet (Sweat). Wit. Samuel Kello, Jr. p. 123

19 June 1797. EDWIN REESE and REBECCA SMITH. Sur. Randolph
Reese. Wit. John D. Haussmann. p. 114

19 January 1809. JOSEPH REESE, JR., and DELILAH PORTER. Sur.
Jacob Williams. Wit. Samuel Kello. Married 24 Jan. by Rev.
Benjamin Barnes, Methodist. p. 188

1 November 1782. RANDOLPH REESE and SALLY HARRIS. Ministers'
returns p. 632

11 November 1792. REUBON (Reuben) REESE and CHARLOTTE HARRISON.
Sur. John Reese. Wit. Samuel Kello. "Reuben" in Ministers'
returns 29 Nov. Married by Rev. Robert Murrell. p. 85

5 January 1793. RIVERS REESE, Son of John Reese, and PIETY
VICK. Sur. Reuben Reese. Wit. Samuel Kello, Andrew Whitehead,
Sally Whitehead and Lotty Reese. p. 86

27 February 1786. ABRAHAM REID and CHARLOTTE BIRD. Ministers'
returns p. 636

25 September 1781. HOLLIDAY REVELL and SALLY WHITFIELD. Sur.
Arthur Doles. p. 31

8 September 1796. JOHN T. RICHARDSON and POLLY NEWSUM, dau.
of Randolph Newsum. Sur. Thomas Newsum. Wit. John D. Haussmann.
p. 109

__ July 1771. JORDAN RICHARDSON and SYLVIA THORPE. Sur. James
Jones. No witness given. p. 16

10 October 1792. JOHN RIDLEY and JANE WRIGHT of age, of North
Carolina. Consent of John Wright brother of Jane. Mother
living but objects to marriage. Sur. John Wright. Wit. John
D. Haussmann, Samuel Kello, John Miles. p. 85

9 April 1778. THOMAS RIDLEY and AMEY SCOTT. Sur. Samuel Kello.
Wit. Richard Kello. p. 26

29 January 1793. CLAXTON ROBERTS and MASON READ, dau. of Sary
Reed. Sur. James Sweat. Wit. John Brooks and Samuel Kello.
Robertson in bond, also Reed. Married 7 Feb. by Rev. Robert
Murrell who says Roberds. p. 88

11 October 1786. HENRY ROBERTSON in bond; Robinson on end of bond; and ELIZABETH LANGSTON. Sur. Thomas Cartner. Wit. Elisha Darden. Married 5 Nov. by Rev. David Barrow who says Robinson. p. 48

22 September 1801. NATHANIEL ROBERTSON and PATIENCE SIMMONS. Sur. John Barnes. Wit. Lewis Bryant. Married 25 Sept. p. 146

21 April 1806. NICHOLAS ROBERTSON and NANCY CUTLER. Sur. John M. Beal. Wit. Bolton Pierce and Ephraim Bryant. Married 28 April by Rev. Benjamin Barnes, Methodist. p. 171

17 February 1791. THOMAS ROBERTSON (Robinson) and PHEBE FAIRCLOTH. Sur. William Vick, Jr. Phoebe in Ministers' returns 24 Feb. Married by Rev. George Gurley, Rector St. Luke's Parish, Episcopal Church. p. 71

31 August 1783. WILLIAM ROBERTSON and ELIZABETH GWYN of Isle of Wight Co. Married by Rev. David Barrow. Ministers' returns p. 637

9 August 1787. LEVI ROCHELLE and SALLY LEWIS. Sur. Moses Foster. p. 52

10 February 1790. COLEN (Collin) ROGERS and MARY CRAFFORD. Sur. Joseph Penrice. Collin in Ministers' returns 12 March. Married by Rev. Robert Murrell. p. 65

18 April 1808. ISHAM ROGERS and POLLY BEAL, dau. of Martha Beal. Sur. John Beal. Wit. Benjamin Cobb. p. 184

12 January 1769. JOHN ROGERS and JUDITH BRICKETT, dau. of James Brickett. Sur. Urwin Browne of Brunswick Co. Wit. Richard Kello. p. 14

19 January 1798. BURWELL ROLLINGS and MARY GREEN. Sur. Augustine C. Cocke. p. 119

20 April 1778. ISAAC ROLLINGS and MARTHA GRAY. Sur. Thomas Lane. Wit. Samuel Kello. p. 26

5 September 1789. JESSE ROLLINS and SUSANNA SCARBOROUGH, consent of Mary Scarborough. Sur. Samuel Stewart. Wit. Samuel Kello. On same bond with Samuel Stewart. p. 62

12 November 1787. BENJAMIN ROSE and LUCY HARPER. Sur. Anselmn Harper. Wit. Samuel Kello. p. 53

MICAJAH ROSE   See William Rose. p. 39

1 June 1795. MICHAEL ROSE and MARTHA BAILEY, dau. of Absalem Bailey. Sur. Samuel Kello. Wit. Rebekah Bailey and Chrischana Fulgem. p. 102

23 January 1785. WILLIAM ROSE and MARY BENNETT. Sur. Moses
M. Phillips. Signed Micajah Rose. p. 39

30 January 1786. JOHN ROSS and MARTHA ONEY. Sur. Arthur Exum.
Wit. Francis Young, Jr. p. 44

17 August 1783. JOHN ROSSER and NANCY LAWRENCE. Ministers'
returns p. 633

7 November 1782. JOHN ROWE and ELIZABETH WOODARD. Ministers'
returns p. 632

23 January 1807. LEMUEL ROWE and REBECCA DENSON. Sur. Drewry
Williams. Wit. Samuel Kello. p. 176

18 December 1776. JOHN RUFFIN and SARAH WILLIAMSON. Sur.
Thomas Williamson. Wit. Drury Andrews. p. 24

17 December 1810. JOHN S. SADLER and SALLY HART. Sur. John
Holleman. Wit. James Rochelle and Tabiah or Silviah Hart.
p. 204

17 January 1804. BRAXTON SAMMONS and POLLY HERN. Married by
Rev. Robert Murrell. Ministers' returns p. 652

30 December 1783. HARDY SAMMONS (Simmons) and CHARLE McLEMORE
ADAMS. Ministers' returns p. 634

2 November 1792. HILL SANDIFORD and JEAN JOHNSON. Sur. Shad
Johnson. Wit. John D. Haussmann. p. 85

14 January 1800. JAMES SANDEFORD and BEEDY WILLSON (Wilson).
Sur. James Willson at top of bond, John Willson at bottom.
Wit. Samuel Kello. Married 15 Jan. by Rev. Benjamin Barnes,
Methodist. p. 132

29 July 1782. JOHN SANDIFUR and PATIENCE BARDEN. Ministers'
returns p. 631

16 May 1782. ROBERT SANDIFUR and NANCY WILLIAMS. Ministers'
returns p. 631

22 June 1762. JOHN SANDS and LUCY NEWSUM, dau. of Thomas
Newsum. Sur. Thomas Atkins (or Atkinson). Wit. Nathaniel
Newsum and Solomon Delouch. p. 7

15 November 1806. ALEXANDER SAUNDERS and NANCY BOYKIN. Sur.
Simon Boykin. p. 174

8 August 1782. BRITAIN SCARBOROUGH and MOLLY CARR. Sur.
Benjamin Stewart. Wit. John Mitchell. Ministers' returns
dated 1 Jan. 1785. p. 33

18 January 1804. HOWELL SCARBROUGH and LUCY SMITH. Sur. Henry Bass and Howell Scarbrough. Wit. N.M. Nance. In the consent the groom is given as Henry Bass. See Henry Bass. p. 158

14 June 1794. JOHN SCARBOROUGH, son of Mary Scarborough, and Phoebe Stuart. Sur. Samuel Kello. Wit. Jesse Rollins. p. 97

19 November 1800. JAMES SCHELL (signature) and NANCY POPE, dau. of Phebe Cahoon. See James Smith. p. 139

24 June 1794. LEWIS SCOGGIN (Coggin) and NANCY BARROTT. Sur. William Mackie (Mackey). p. 97

11 May 1785. GODFREY SCOTT and BETSEY FRANCIS. Married by Rev. David Barrow. Ministers' returns p. 638

16 November 1795. GODFREY SCOTT and TABITHA BYRD, Sarah Read mother of Tabitha, father of Tabitha is dead. Sur. Cordall Read. Wit. John D. Haussmann. Married 22 Nov. by Rev. Robert Murrell. p. 104

-- December 1785. SAMUEL SCARBROUGH and LYDIA HINES (Lydia Harris on back of bond). Ministers' returns 29 Dec. Sur. Britain Scarbrough. p. 43

1 September 1783. THEOPHILUS SCOTT and MARY VASSER. Sur. Thomas Ridley and John Scott. Wit. Nicholas Maget. p. 37

24 June 1786. JOHN SCREWS and HOLLAND BENNETT. Sur. Britain Johnson. Married 29 June by Rev. David Barrow. p. 46

16 March 1807. RICHARD SCUTCHINGS and CATHARINE GARDNER. Sur. Jacob Beal. Wit. Benjamin Cobb. p. 178'

30 September 1758. BENJAMIN SEBRELL and ANN MORRICE, dau. of Nicholas Morris. Sur. Samuel Sands. Wit. Richard Kello, Daniel Sebrell and Margaret Sebrell. p. 4

-- November 1801. JAMES SEBRELL and NANCY SIMMONS. Sur. Edwin Simmons. p. 147

25 October 1808. NICHOLAS SEBRELL and BETSY EDMUNDS. Sur. Benjamin Cobb. Wit. James Rochelle, Betsy Lewis and William Saunders. p. 186

30 November 1797. RICHARD SHARP and POLLY HUNTER, dau. of Emanuel Hunter. Sur. John Pledger. Wit. Samuel Kello. p. 117

25 August 1800. RICHARD SHARP and PATSY POPE. Sur. Benjamin Johnson. Wit. Samuel Kello, Jr. p. 137

24 July 1809. JOHN SHEPHERD, JR. and MRS. SUSAN LUNDY. Sur. Charles B. Nicholson. Wit. John Myrick "of Owen". p. 193

SHERWOOD.   See Sherard

27 November 1791. ARTHUR SHERWOOD and SARAH BOYKIN. Married by Rev. George Gurley, Rector of St. Luke's Parish, Episcopal Church. Ministers' returns p. 646.   See Arthur Sherard

10 November 1791. ARTHUR SHERARD and SARAH BOYKIN. Sur. John Boykin. Wit. John D. Haussmann. Sherwood in Ministers' returns 27 Nov. See Arthur Sherwood. p. 76

18 March 1805. JOHN SHIELD and SALLY WILLIAMSON. Sur. George Branch. Wit. Samuel Kello. p. 165

13 July 1769. JOHN SIMMONDS (Simmons) and LUCY SIMMONDS (Simmons). John son of Charles Simmons. Sur. John Simmons, Sr. Wit. Richard Kello. p. 14

13 November 1790. _____ SIMMONS and SARAH EDMUNDS, dau. of Karenhappuch Edmunds. This is consent only. p. 68

12 February 1756. CHARLES SIMMONS and MARY WAINWRIGHT. Sur. Richard Kello. Wit. Benjamin Simmons. p. 2

19 December 1795. CHARLES SIMMONS and HANNAH DREWRY. Sur. Samuel Kello. Wit. Spratley Simmons. p. 105

22 September 1788. DANIEL SIMMONS and MARY GRAY, dau. of Edwin Gray. Sur. Samuel Kello. p. 56

17 March 1785. EDWIN SIMMONS and REBECCA SIMMONS. Ministers' returns p. 635

28 December 1804. EDWIN SIMMONS and POLLEY WILLIAMS. Sur. James Barrett. Wit. Bolton Pierce. p. 164

12 January 1786. HENRY SIMMONS and REBECCA ANDREWS. Sur. Samuel Kello. p. 44

25 November 1790. JAMES SIMMONS and SALLY EDMUNDS. Married by Rev. Robert Murrell. p. 646

29 December 1761. JOHN SIMMONS and LUCY THORPE (Thorp), dau. of Timothy Thorp. Sur. Kinchen Taylor. Wit. Richard Kello. p. 6

12 June 1766. JOHN SIMMONS and SUSANNA JONES. Sur. James Jones. Wit. Edward Fisher. p. 11

12 January 1786. JOHN SIMMONS and PATIENCE JACKSON. Ministers' returns p. 636

18 September 1797. PETER SIMMONS and MARGARET DREW. Sur. Frederick Parker. Wit. Samuel Kello. p. 115

13 September 1787. SPRATLEY SIMMONS and ANNA DRURY. Sur. Samuel Drury (Drewry). Wit. Richard Kello. p. 52

6 August 1782. THOMAS SIMMONS and LUCY CLEMENTS, dau. of George Clements, deceased. Sur. Arthur Boykin who is guardian of Lucy. Wit. Richard Kello. p. 33

-- June 1798. VALENTINE SIMMONS and TEMPERANCE ATKINSON, no parents living and she is of age. Sur. William Bryant. Wit. Samuel Kello, Jr., and William Bryant, Jr. p. 121

-- January 1758. WILLIAM SIMMONS and SARAH BUTTS. Sur. John Simmons. p. 4

9 September 1790. WILLIAM SIMMONS and JANE LEWIS, dau. of Mary Lewis. Sur. Francis Young, Jr. Wit. Joseph Ruffin and Levy Rochell. p. 67

11 May 1803. WILLIAM SIMMONS, SR., and TEMPERANCE MURFEE. Sur. Benjamin Kirby. Wit. James Sebrell. p. 154

15 August 1803. WILLIAM SIMMONS and ELIZABETH NEWSUM. Sur. Nathaniel Newsum. p. 155

8 September 1774. JAMES SKINNER and MARTHA ELIZABETH WILKINSON. Sur. James and John Wilkinson. p. 21

21 July 1792. JETHRO SLADE and MARY HARRIS. Sur. Samuel Slade. Wit. Samuel Kello. p. 83

16 July 1810. JOHN P. SLADE and TEMPERANCE A. POND. Sur. Samuel Pond. Wit. Samuel Kello. Married 1 Aug. by Rev. Drewry Lane. p. 201

4 February 1805. SAMUEL SLADE and _____ GAY. Sur. Thomas Chappell. Wit. Bolton Pierce. p. 165

27 December 1806. HENRY SLEDGE and SARAH IVEY, JR., dau. of George Ivey, Sr. Sur. George Ivey, Jr. Wit. Samuel Kello. p. 175

14 September 1792. STERLING SLEDGE and ANNA (Annis) WIGGINS, consent of Abraham Wiggins and Annis Wiggins. Sur. John Sledge. Wit. Samuel Kello. p. 84

12 July 1762. ISHAM SMITH and PATIENCE DREW, dau. of Newit Drew. Sur. James Jones. Wit. Richard Kello and William Parham. p. 7

19 May 1788. JAMES SMITH and NANCY NORVELL. Sur. William Smith. Wit. Kinchen Turner. p. 55

19 November 1800. JAMES SMITH, at top, center and back of bond, JAMES SCHELL his signature, and NANCY POPE. Phiba Cahoon mother of Nancy. Sur. Miles Cary. Wit. Samuel Kello. (Note: Jeremiah Cahoon married Phebe Pope 12 Feb. 1799.) See James Schell. p. 139

10 October 1795. NATHANIEL SMITH and LUCY LUNDY, dau. of Elizabeth Lundy who consents. Sur. William Clark. Wit. Samuel Kello and Henry Knight. Married 22 Oct. by Rev. Robert Murrell. p. 103

14 June 1783. WILLIAM SMITH and ELIZABETH TAYLOR. Sur. Samuel Kello. p. 36

3 February 1793. WILLIAM SMITH and TEMPERANCE WESTBROOK. Married by Rev. Robert Murrell. Ministers' returns p. 647

24 September 1788. CHARLES SPEED and JEAN DOYEL. Sur. John Stephenson. Wit. Samuel Kello. p. 56

1 March 1791. HENRY SPEED and BETSEY SPEED, dau. of Ann Speed. Sur. Richard Johnson. Wit. John D. Haussmann and Samuel Kello. Married 3 Mar. by Rev. George Gurley, Rector of St. Luke's Parish, Episcopal Church. p. 72

21 December 1790. WILLIAM SPEED and FANNY HUNTER. Sur. Micajah Stevens (bottom of bond, Charles Stevens at top of bond). Wit. Samuel Kello. 8 Jan. 1791 in Ministers' returns. Married by Rev. George Gurley, Rector of St. Luke's Parish, Episcopal Church. p. 69

18 March 1786. DAVID SPENCER and MARY WILLSON, of St. Luke's Parish dau. of John and Susannah Willson. Drury Beel guardian of David. Sur. Jacob Bailey. Wit. Richard Kello. p. 45

9 November 1782. JESSE SPENCER and RACHEL DAUGHTRY. Ministers' returns p. 632

23 October 1799. WILLIAM SPENCER and CROESA (Crisey) FIERS, dau. of William and Sally Fier. Sur. John Vick. "Creesa" in Ministers' returns 24 Oct. Married by Rev. Benjamin Barnes, Methodist. p. 129

25 December 1788. JOHN SPIVEY, under age, son of William Spivey, and PHOEBE ADAMS, dau. of John Adams who is surety. Wit. Samuel Kello. p. 57

15 July 1764. WILLIAM T. SPIVEY and DOROTHY VASSER of Nottoway Parish. Sur. Benjamin Exum. Wit. Edward Fisher. p. 9

2 June 1810. THOMAS SPIVY and CHASTITY WASHINGTON. Sur. Richard Vick. Wit. Joseph Bracey and Samuel Kello. p. 200

31 October 1797. SAMUEL STANTON and RACHEL NICHOLSON, widow of William Nicholson, deceased, dau. of George Blunt. Sur. Moses Stanton. Wit. Samuel Kello, Jr., and Thomas Nicholson. Married 4 Nov. by Rev. Drewry Lane. p. 116

17 May 1806. LEMUEL STEPHENS and ELIZABETH (Betsy) JORDAN.
Sur. Joel Waddill. Wit. Benjamin Cobb and Keton Pope. Married
18 May by Rev. Exum Everett. p. 171

19 November 1810. MARTIN STEPHENS and LUCY WOODWARD. Sur.
Thadeus Powell. Wit. Samuel Kello and Harrison Minton. See
Martin Stephenson. p. 203

30 June 1809. WILLIAM STEPHENS and OLIVE WILLSON. Sur. Rueben
Whitfield. Wit. Samuel Kello. See William Stephenson. p. 193

11 November 1800. AMOS STEPHENSON and PRUDENCE FRANCIS. Sur.
Asa Beal. Wit. Samuel Kello, Jr. Married 12 Nov. by Rev.
Benjamin Barnes, Methodist. p. 139

30 August 1796. CHARLES STEPHENSON and PATSEY WILLIAMS. Sur.
Matthew Stephenson. Wit. Samuel Kello. p. 109

23 May 1809. CHARLES STEPHENSON and ANN KINDRED. Sur. John
Carr. Wit. Harrison Minton. Married 1 June by Rev. Benjamin
Barnes, Methodist. p. 191

7 June 1791. GEORGE STEPHENSON and PHEBE (?) WESTBROOK. Sur.
Samuel Kello. p. 74

17 January 1803. HARRISON STEPHENSON and POLLY HANCOCK, dau.
of Sally Hancock. Sur. Jesse Stephenson. p. 152

24 March 1792. JAMES STEPHENSON and SALLY WOMBWELL, on face
of bond - Womble on back of bond. Sur. William Stephenson.
Wit. John D. Haussmann. p. 81

30 April 1807. JESSE STEPHENSON and MARIANNA WILLIAMSON.
Married by Rev. Drewry Lane. Ministers' returns p. 654

16 July 1804. JOHN STEPHENSON and MILLY BRITE (Britte). Sur.
Willis Stephenson. Wit. Benjamin Cobb, Samuel Kello. p. 161.

19 February 1810. JOHN STEPHENSON and REBECCA SUMMERELL. Sur.
Jesse Branch. Wit. Lesay Summerell and James Rochelle. p. 198

17 March 1785. LEMUEL STEPHENSON and ELIZABETH WARREN.
Ministers' returns p. 635

19 November 1810. MARTIN STEPHENSON and LUCY WOODWARD. Sur.
Thadeus Powell. Wit. Samuel Kello and Harrison Minton. See
Martin Stephens. p. 203

19 August 1805. MILLS STEPHENSON and JULIA ADAMS, consent of
Molly Adams. Sur. Robert Adams. Wit. B. Coan. p. 166

25 October 1796. NATHANIEL STEPHENSON and NANCY SHIELD. Sur. Robert Stevenson. Wit. Samuel Kello. p. 110

10 February 1808. SAMUEL STEPHENSON and POLLY STEPHENSON (Stevens). Sur. Valentine Jenkins. Wit. Samuel Kello. p. 182

18 October 1792. WILLIAM STEPHENSON, JR., and LUCY BRISTER, of age. Sur. Stephen Summerell. Wit. Samuel Kello and Samuel Brister. p. 85

30 June 1809. WILLIAM STEPHENSON and OLIVE WILLSON. Sur. Reuben Whitfield. Wit. Samuel Kello. Married 2 July by Rev. Benjamin Barnes, Methodist, who says Wilson. See William Stevens. p. 193

20 December 1802. WILLIS STEPHENSON and SALLY WEST. Sur. William West. Wit. Benjamin Cobb. p. 151

1 October 1785. MATTHEW STEVENS and ELIZABETH HAZELWOOD. Sur. Daniel Doyel. Wit. Samuel Kello. p. 41

18 October 1787. MICHAEL STEVENS and ANNA JOYNER. Sur. Silas Louve (Love). Stevenson in Ministers' returns 23 Oct. See Michael Stevenson. p. 53

23 October 1787. MICHAEL STEVENSON and ANN JOYNER. Married by Rev. D.C. Barrow. See Michael Stevens. Ministers' returns p. 640

10 January 1805. ROBERT STEVENSON and JANE JOHNSON. Married by Rev. Drewry Lane. Ministers' returns p. 654

23 January 1788. THOMAS STEVENSON and NANCY PLEDGER. Sur. Arthur Doles. p. 54

12 December 1764. RICHARD STEWART of Brunswick Co., and ANN MYRICK, dau. of John and Ann Myrick. Sur. Owen Myrick. Wit. Richard Kello and James Barnes. p. 10

7 June 1808. RICHARD STEWART and MARTHA MILLAR. Sur. Benjamin Millar. Wit. Benjamin Cobb. p. 185

5 September 1789. SAMUEL STEWART and PHOEBE ROLLINS. Sur. Jesse Rollins. Wit. Samuel Kello. On same bond with Jesse Rollins. p. 62

11 August 1806. GRIFFIN STITH and MARGARET BOUSH, dau. of A. Jones who says Margaret Bouth. Sur. Joshua Fort. Wit. Benjamin Cobb and Samuel Kello. p. 172

19 February 1791. THOMAS STOKES and UNITY CAREY. Sur. David Edwards. Wit. John D. Haussmann. p. 71

21 November 1808. JOHN STOREY and ANNA VICK. Sur. William Cutler. Wit. Samuel Kello. p. 187

12 January 1810. CHARLES STORY and LYDIA WHITEHEAD, dau. of
Sally Knox. Sur. Isaac M. Knox. Married 14 Jan. by Rev. Exum
Everett. p. 197

12 April 1781. DANIEL STORY and ELIZABETH SPEED. Sur. Jerry
Drake. p. 30

26 February 1788. JAMES STORY and ESTHER WILLSON, dau. of
John and Susannah Willson. Sur. John Beal. Wit. Samuel Kello.
p. 55

15 December 1800. JESSE STORY center of bond, JESSE POPE top,
bottom and back of bond; and NANCY STORY. Sur. Benjamin Johnston.
Wit. Samuel Kello, Jr. Jesse Pope and Nancy Story in ministers'
returns 18 Dec. 1800. See Jesse Pope. p. 140

8 November 1808. JESSE STORY and PATSY NEWBY. Sur. Zecheus
Story. Wit. Benjamin Cobb. p. 187

15 January 1785. JOHN STORY and JANET BRITT. Ministers'
returns p. 635

17 December 1810. AZCHEUS STORY and BEDY STORY, dau. of James
and Hester Story. Sur. Samuel Story. Wit. James Rochelle.
p. 204

1 December 1798. JOHN STRAUD and AMEY STRICLING (Stricktling).
Sur. William Crichlow. Wit. Samuel Kello, Jr. p. 123

10 February 1796. JOHN STRICKLAND and CHARLOTTE CAMBELL. Sur.
Allen Boon. Wit. Benjamin Blunt, Winny Cook, William Jackson
and Batt Boon. p. 106

16 November 1807. WILLIAM H. SULLIVAN and MARGARET BARHAM.
Sur. Howd. Barham. p. 180

9 August 1786. GEORGE SUMMERELL and ELIZABETH COOPER. Sur.
Arthur Doles. Wit. Francis Young, Jr. Married by Rev. David
Barrow on 18 Aug. p. 46

6 October 1806. HAROD SUMMERELL and SALLY HAIL. Sur. Jesse
Lowe. Wit. Samuel Kello. p. 173

11 November 1790. HENRY SUMMERELL and DIZEY HOLDING. Sur.
Benjamin Branch. Wit. Samuel Kello. p. 68

14 November 1770. JAMES SUMMERELL, son of George Summerell, and
ANNA CALTHORPE of Nottoway Parish. Edmund Tyler guardian of
Anna. Sur. Anthony Calthorpe. Wit. Richard Kello, Newson
Branch, Mary Branch and Charles Poers. p. 16

30 January 1792. JEREMIAH SUMMERELL and THAMER BRITT. Sur.
William Stevenson (Stephenson). Wit. Samuel Kello. p. 78

29 April 1782. JOHN SUMMERELL and SARAH BRITT. Sur. Arthur
Boykin. Wit. Richard Kello. p. 32

12 June 1778. STEPHEN SUMMERELL and RUTH BRISTOW, both of
Nottoway Parish; Ruth dau. of Samuel Bristow. Sur. Boaz Gevin
Summerill. Wit. Samuel Kello. p. 26

19 August 1791. THOMAS SUMMERELL and MARTHA HOUGH. Sur. William
Stephenson. Wit. John D. Haussmann. p. 74

5 January 1793. WILLIAM SUMMERELL and ELIZABETH WILLIAMS. Sur.
Arthur Boykin. Wit. John D. Haussmann. p. 87

3 March 1800. WILLIAM SUMMERELL and ELIZABETH SHIELD. Sur.
Thomas Summerell. Wit. Samuel Kello and Thomas Summerell, Jr.
p. 134

29 December 1798. WILLSON SUMMERELL and LIEURANER HOLDEN, free
by age, without any gargent (guardian?). Sur. Solomon Cooper.
Married by Rev. Drewry Lane. p. 124

12 May 1768. JOHN SUTER and HANNAH SMITH. Sur. Stephen
Williamson. Wit. John Dawson. p. 13

3 March 1790. JAMES SWEAT and PATIENCE READ, dau. of John and
Sarah Read. Sur. David Read. Wit. Samuel Kello and Cordall
Read. p. 65

21 April 1800. JAMES TALLER, of Isle of Wight Co., and LYDIA
WILLIAMS, dau. of William Williams, Sr. Sur. William Williams,
Jr. Wit. Samuel Kello. p. 135

21 July 1806. JAMES TALLOW and DELILAH BEEL. Sur. William
Williams. Wit. Rice B. Pierc. p. 172

24 January 1807. SAMUEL TANNER and JANE FOSTER. Sur. Henry
Banks. Wit. Samuel Kello. p. 177

21 November 1803. THOMAS TANNER and FANNY CLAUD. Sur. James
Simmons. Wit. Samuel Kello. Married 15 Dec. by Rev. Robert
Murrell. p. 157

5 March 1792. BATTS TATUM and SALLY B. THORPE, consent of
Lucy Thorp. Sur. John Williamson. Wit. John D. Haussmann,
John Thorp, Charles B. Nicolson. p. 80

8 May 1809. EDWARD TATUM and HANNAH MORRIS. Sur. James
Gilliam. Wit. Bolling Barnes and Samuel Kello. p. 191

2 April 1782. BARTON TAYLOR and SALLY ATKINSON, dau. of James
Atkinson. Sur. Mike Edwards. Wit. James Atkinson. p. 32

10 December 1786. EDWARD TAYLOR and SELAH McCLENNY. Married
by Rev. David Barrow. Ministers' returns p. 639

-- June 1782. ETHELDRED TAYLOR and REBECCA TYUS (Tyns?). Sur. Jeremiah Tyus (Tyns). Wit. Samuel Kello. p. 33

26 February 1798. HENRY TAYLOR and REBECCA CLAUD. Sur. John Taylor, Jr. Wit. Samuel Kello, Jr., and A. Parker. p. 119

10 May 1781. JAMES TAYLOR and ELIZABETH MURRAY, dau. of Alexander Murray who is surety. p. 30

6 May 1808. JAMES TAYLOR and MARY COBB. Sur. Edwin Boykin. Wit. Samuel Kello. p. 184

5 August 1783. JOHN TAYLOR and SARAH RUFFIN (widow). Sur. Richard Kello. Wit. Samuel Kello. p. 36

3 March 1785. JOHN TAYLOR and MARTHA PATERSON. Ministers' returns p. 635

25 December 1797. JOHN TAYLOR and ARRY WILLIAMS. Sur. Samuel Clark. Wit. Richard Kello. p. 118

19 January 1807. LEWIS TAYLOR and PEGGY CARY. Sur. Samuel Blunt. Wit. Benjamin Cobb. Married 22 Jan. by Rev. James Rogers. p. 176

19 April 1788. THOMAS TAYLOR and REBECCA GRAY, both of Surry County. Married by Rev. D.C. Barrow. Ministers' returns p. 640

12 February 1753. LITTLETON TAZEWELL of Brunswick Co., and Mary Gray. Sur. Benjamin Ruffin of Surry. Wit. Richard Kello. p. 1

16 December 1796. DAVID THOMAS and NANCY HARRISON. Sur. Briggs Nowell. Wit. John D. Haussmann and Henry Harrison. p. 112

20 September 1803. DAVID THOMAS and GINCEY (Geney) WOMACK. Sur. Henry Harrison. Wit. Briggs Norvell. p. 156

15 September 1801. EDWARD THOMAS and TERESA RICKS. Sur. Peter Joe. Wit. Samuel Kello, Jr. p. 146

14 November 1755. HENRY THOMAS and MARTHA JARRELL (widow). Sur. Micajah Edwards. Wit. Richard Kello. p. 2

8 November 1786. ISHAM THOMAS and SARAH CROCHER. Sur. John Tann. Wit. Francis Young, Jr. and Belah Welleford. p. 48

24 December 1783. MATHEW THOMAS and SELAH HOLLAND, both of Nansemond Co., and came over in absence of those who were licensed to marry in that county. Married by Rev. David Barrow. Ministers' returns p. 637

12 March 1795. NATHAN THOMAS and CATHARINE GRAY, dau. of Hannah Gray. Sur. Etheldred Turner. Wit. John D. Haussmann. Married 2 April by Rev. Robert Murrell. p. 101

4 March 1789. SAMPSON THOMAS and BETTY GARNER. Sur. James Blackshins. Wit. Samuel Kello. On same bond with James Blackshins. Married 13 March by Rev. D.C. Barrow. p. 58

18 September 1799. WILLIAM THOMPSON and PATIENCE SIMMONS. Sur. Ephraim Bryant. Wit. Samuel Kello, Jr. p. 128

15 December 1800. WILLIAM THORN and POLLY DOYAL. Sur. Peter Boothe. Married 25 Dec. by Rev. Burwell Barrett. p. 140

12 January 1797. HARDY THORPE and MARY THOMAS. Sur. Robert Mabry. p. 113

20 February 1783. HENRY THORPE and PRISCILLA HARRIS. Ministers' returns p. 632

21 February 1781. JOHN THORPE and MARY REECE. Ministers' returns p. 630

13 November 1771. LEWIS THORPE and ELIZABETH SIMMONS, dau. of Benjamin Simmons. Sur. Benjamin Sinnons, Jr. Wit. Samuel Kello. p. 17

7 November 1809. LEWIS THORPE, JR. and MASON S. WESTBROOK. Jane Westbrook guardian of Mason S. Sur. Benjamin Simmons. Wit. James Rochell and John Thorpe. p. 195

9 November 1769. MOSES THORPE and SARAH SEWARD. Sur. Joshua Nicholson. Wit. Richard Kello. p. 15

12 December 1776. HENRY TILLER (Tillar) and ELIZABETH RIVES. Sur. Major Tiller. Wit. Samuel Kello. p. 24

5 September 1779. HENRY TILLER and CHRISTIAN LUNDY. Sur. Major Tiller. Wit. Samuel Kello. p. 28

9 February 1792. JOHN TILLAR and REBECCA WESTBROOK, dau. of Henry Westbrook. Sur. Kirby Bittle. Wit. John D. Haussmann. p. 78

2 October 1783. WILLIAM TOMLINSON and REBECCA STEWART. Ministers' returns p. 633

11 July 1801. EDWIN TRAVIS and MARY H. ROGERS. Sur. John George. Wit. Samuel Kello, Jr., Martha Lane, Catharine Travis. Married by Rev. William Hargrave who says _Polly_. p. 145

10 April 1801. CAPT. STITH TUCKER and POLLY GILLIAM, dau. of Thomas Gilliam. Sur. John Gilliam. Wit. Samuel Kello. p. 144

25 January 1792. JOHN TUNNELL and ELIZABETH HARRIS. Sur. William W. Spooner. Wit. Samuel Kello and John D. Haussmann. Tunnel in Ministers' returns 29 Jan. Married by Rev. Robert Murrell. She must have been a widow for on 18 May 1802, Jesse Holt m. Jane Harris, dau. of Elizabeth Tunnel. p. 78

3 January 1799. WILLIAM TUNNELL and BETSY LITTLE. Sur. Enos James. Wit. Samuel Kello, Jr. p. 124

26 April 1781. ARTHUR TURNER and NANCY LEWIS, dau. of Benjamin Lewis, consent of Thomas Turner. Sur. Littleton Turner. Wit. Richard Kello. p. 30

26 March 1799. BARDEN (Burden) TURNER and ELIZABETH BRADSHAW. Sur. William Bradshaw. Wit. Samuel Kello. p. 126

30 May 1781. BENJAMIN TURNER and MARY GRIFFIN. Thomas Holladay guardian of Mary. Sur. Turner Kirby. Wit. Samuel Kello. p. 30

10 January 1809. BENJAMIN TURNER and ELIZA BOYKIN. Married by Rev. Benjamin Barnes, Methodist. Ministers' returns p. 658

13 April 1791. CALEB TURNER and PHERIBA (Pheruby) TURNER. Sur. Samuel Turner, consent of Joshua Turner. Wit. John D. Haussmann. p. 73

25 September 1783. DAVID TURNER and FANNY JOYNER. Married by Rev. David Barrow. Ministers' returns p. 637

20 December 1801. DAVID TURNER and SALLY HARRIS. Sur. William Kirby. Wit. Edmund Turner. p. 148

6 November 1806. DAVID TURNER and LUCY JOHNSON, dau. of Council Johnson. Sur. John Denson. Wit. Samuel Kello and Ro. Denson. p. 174

13 November 1787. EDMUND TURNER and REBECCA DAWSON. Sur. William Edmunds. p. 53

9 February 1802. ETHELDRED TURNER and CHERRY JOHNSON. Sur. Henry Turner. p. 149

28 February 1799. EVERITT TURNER and BETSEY DAVIS, dau. of Lewis Davis. Sur. John Doyell. p. 125

8 March 1787. HARRIS TURNER and REBECCA GEE. Sur. John Barrow. Wit. Francis Young, Jr. and James Lundy. Married 20 Mar. by Rev. George Gurley, Rector of St. Luke's Parish, Episcopal Church. p. 51

22 December 1778. HENRY TURNER and WILLEATHBY HARRIS. Sur. Littleton Turner. Wit. Thomas Turner and Priscilla McElmore. p. 27

3 May 1783. HENRY TURNER and MILLE BITTLE. Sur. John Barrow.
Wit. Robert Bittle and Samuel Kello. p. 36

2 June 1754. JACOB TURNER and MARY BLUNT, dau. of Priscilla
Blunt. Sur. Henry Crafford. Wit. Richard Kello, J. Baker, Jr.,
W. Blunt and William Bynum. Mary in bond - Anne in consent.
Anne in division of her father Benjamin Blunt's slaves. p. 2

14 September 1801. JACOB TURNER and MARGARET SAPHEN, Carrstrphen
in her consent. Sur. Micajah Griffin. p. 146

8 September 1810. JACOB TURNER, SR. and WINNEY CRUMPLER. Sur.
Simon Boykin. Wit. William Crumpler and James Rochelle. p. 202

14 October 1784. JAMES TURNER and REBECCA TURNER. Consent
only. Ministers' returns dated 30 Nov. p. 39

14 January 1786. JAMES TURNER and FRANCES BETTS. Sur. Beverley
Booth. Wit. Francis Young, Jr. p. 44

11 February 1762. JOHN TURNER and PRISCILLA BLUNT, dau. of
Priscilla Blunt. Sur. John Blunt. Wit. Richard Kello and
William Blunt. p. 7

11 February 1790. JOSEPH TURNER and LUCY WESTBROOK. Married
by Rev. Robert Murrell. Ministers' returns p. 646

9 April 1801. JOSEPH TURNER and POLLEY SMITH. Ministers'
returns p. 652

14 October 1790. KINCHEN TURNER and FRANCES DRURY (Drewry).
John Rogers guardian of Frances. Sur. Jesse Holt. Wit. John
Rogers and Mary Norwell. p. 67

21 November 1808. LEMUEL TURNER and ELIZABETH JOINER. Sur.
Jeremiah Joyner. Wit. Benjamin Cobb. p. 187

16 June 1806. MILLS TURNER and CHARLOTTE BLYTHE, dau. of
Elizabthe Eligh who consents. Sur. Nathan Johnson. Wit. Bolton
Pierce and Ro. Denson. p. 171

5 February 1800. NATHAN TURNER and SALLY DREWRY. Sur. Thomas
Willeford. Wit. Samuel Kello, Jr. p. 133

11 September 1787. PIERCE TURNER and BETTY POWELL. Married
by Rev. David Barrow. Ministers' returns p. 639

17 February 1784. SAMUEL TURNER and SALLY LEWIS. Married by
Rev. David Barrow. Ministers' returns p. 637

22 September 1806. SAMUEL TURNER and ESTHER W. FRANCIS.
Married by Rev. Benjamin Barnes, Methodist. Ministers' returns
p. 657

9 October 1766. SIMON TURNER and LUCY LITTLE (widow). Sur.
William Person. Wit. Richard Kello and Thomas Person, Jr.
John Little m. Lucy Bittle 22 July 1758. He died 1764. p. 11

6 December 1767. SIMON TURNER of Brunswick Co., and ANN
WILLIAMSON of Nottoway Parish. Sur. William Williamson. Wit.
Richard Kello. p. 12

2 January 1798. SOLOMON TURNER and POLLY HOLMES. Sur. Solomon
(Job) Holmes. Wit. Samuel Kello. p. 118

15 January 1773. THOMAS TURNER and MARY LEWIS, dau. of Benjamin
Lewis. Sur. Benjamin Turner. Wit. William Turner and Richard
Kello. p. 19

15 April 1777. THOMAS TURNER and CHARLOTTE HARRIS, dau. of
Edward and Elizabeth Harris. Sur. William Turner. Wit. Samuel
Kello. p. 24

18 February 1793. THOMAS TURNER and LUCY BETTS. Sur. Valentine
Jenkins. Wit. John D. Haussmann. p. 88

20 November 1809. THOMAS B. TURNER and TEMPERANCE HARRIS.
Sur. David Myrick. Wit. Samuel Kello. p. 195

10 December 1795. WILLIAM TURNER and MILDRED TURNER. Sur.
William Turner, Jr. Wit. John D. Haussmann. p. 104

27 January 1794. WILLIS TURNER, son of John Turner, and
ELIZABETH POPE. Sur. Ephraim Turner and Samuel Turner. Wit.
Richard Kello. p. 94

10 August 1758. EDMUND TYLER and SARAH CALTHORP. Sur. Daniel
Fisher. Wit. Thomas Blunt. p. 4

4 November 1799. EDWARD WASHINGTON TYLER and MARTHA ADAMS.
Sur. James Clayton. p. 129

7 February 1783. JEREMIAH TYLER and ELIZABETH JARRELL.
Albridgton Jones guardian of Elizabeth Jarrell. Sur. James
Cosby. Wit. Samuel Kello. Elizabeth probably dau. of Benjamin
and Mary (Jones) Jarrell: Benjamin Jarrell died 1769. Albridgton Jones was Elizabeth's grandfather. p. 35

21 December 1807. TIMOTHY TYNES and REBECCA BRITT, dau. of
Nancy Britt. Sur. Henry Tynes. p. 181

11 April 1764. ABSALOM TYUS (Tyns?) of Sussex Co., and SYLVIA
WILLIAMSON. Sur. Absalom Williamson. Wit. Richard Kello.
Must be Tyus as an Absalom Tyus died in Sussex 177-. Torrence's
Wills p. 432. p. 9

1 March 1762. BENJAMIN TYUS of Sussex Co., and ELIZABETH
WILLIAMSON. Sur. Absalam Williamson. Wit. Edward Fisher and
Jonathan Godwin. p. 7

5 November 1803. JACOB UNDERWOOD and ELIZABETH ADAMS. Sur.
Robert Brittle. Wit. Samuel Kello. p. 156

24 March 1807. WILLIE UNDERWOOD and MARTHA M. BITTLE. Sur.
John T. Vaughan. Wit. Henry Bittle and Samuel Kello. p. 178

10 December 1792. JOHN URQUHART and NANCY WILLIAMSON. Sur.
Micajah Holliman. p. 86

12 August 1772. WILLIAM URQUHART and MARY SIMMONS. Sur.
Samuel Kello. Wit. J. Gray and Richard Kello. p. 18

18 August 1790. JAMES UZZELL and LYDIA BOOLS. Sur. John
Lankford. Wit. Francis Young, Jr. p. 66

9 September 1782. CHURCH VALENTINE and JULIA FLEMING. Ministers'
returns p. 631

28 October 1786. ETHELDRED VASSER and MARY CLARKE. Sur.
James Calthorpe. Wit. Francis Young, Jr. p. 48

14 April 1791. JESSE VASSER and SUSANNA HART, dau. of William
Hart who is surety. Wit. John D. Haussmann. Susannah in
Ministers' returns 15 May. Married by Rev. George Gurley,
Rector of St. Luke's Parish, Episcopal Church. p. 73

8 March 1787. HENRY VAUGHAN and LYDIA VICK, consent of Patty
Vaughan as to Henry, and consent of Shadrack Vick as to Lyida.
Sur. Robert Williams. Wit. Francis Young, Jr. Married by Rev.
George Gurley, Rector of St. Luke's Parish, Episcopal Church.
p. 51

20 February 1792. HENRY VAUGHAN and RHODA EDWARDS. Sur. Edwin
Edwards. Wit. John D. Haussmann. p. 79

31 July 1806. HENRY VAUGHAN and POLLY EDWARDS, dau. of James
Edwards. Sur. Albridgton Edwards. Wit. Samuel Kello and Rice
B. Pierce. p. 172

12 December 1810. HENRY VAUGHAN and TEMPERANCE WILLS. Sur.
James Wills. Wit. Harrison Minton. p. 203

11 October 1770. JAMES VAUGHAN and PHEBY (Phebe) CROCKER,
dau. of Benjamin Crocker. Sur. William Millar. Consent of
Sarah Crocker. p. 16

8 May 1794. JOEL VAUGHAN and SALLY PAINE. Sur. Basil Paine.
Wit. John D. Haussmann. p. 96

17 December 1807. JOHN T. VAUGHAN and MARTHA N. FOSTER, grand
dau. of Arthur Foster. Sur. Benjamin Barnes. Wit. Samuel Kello.
Married 24 Dec. by Rev. Benjamin Barnes, Methodist. p. 181

29 March 1781. SEYMORE VAUGHAN and AMEY COBB (widow). Ministers' returns p. 630

15 January 1805. SEYMOUR VAUGHAN and BETSEY WILLS. Sur. Thomas Wills. Wit. Samuel Kello. In same bond with Thomas Wills. p. 164

4 November 1803. SHADRACH VAUGHAN and CHARITY WELLS. Sur. Albridgton Edwards. Wit. Samuel Kello. p. 156

31 October 1782. THOMAS VAUGHAN and SALLY JONES. Ministers' returns p. 631

20 October 1804. THOMAS VAUGHAN, JR. and REBECCA FOSTER, dau. of Arthur Foster. Thomas Vaughan, Sr. guardian of Thomas Vaughan, Jr. Consent only. Wit. Samuel Kello. Married 21 Oct. by Rev. Benjamin Barnes, Methodist. p. 162

13 May 1774. WILLIAM VAUGHAN son of Henry Vaughan, and ANN POPE. Edmund Day guardian of Ann. Sur. Richard Blow and James Taylor. Wit. Richard Kello, Jr., Robert Washington and Howell Vaughan. p. 21

21 March 1802. BENJAMIN VICK and SALLY DAVIS. Sur. Amos Gardner. Wit. Samuel Kello. p. 150

31 December 1807. ELISHA VICK and NANCY JOINER. Sur. John Revell. Wit. Benjamin Cobb. Married by Rev. Benjamin Barnes, Methodist. p. 181

25 March 1799. EXUM VICK and PEGGY VICK. Sur. Nathan English. Wit. Samuel Kello, Jr. Married 28 March by Rev. Benjamin Barnes, Methodist. p. 126

8 August 1797. JAMES VICK and LYDIA JOINER. Married by Rev. Benjamin Barnes, Methodist. Ministers' returns p. 648

21 January 1789. JOEL VICK and JULIA DOYEL. Sur. Hardy Doyel. Wit. Samuel Kello. Married by Rev. George Gurley, Rector of St. Luke's Parish, Episcopal Church. p. 58

19 February 1810. JOEL VICK and JINCEY VICK. Sur. Joel Vick. Wit. Harrison Minton. Married 16 March by Rev. Benjamin Barnes, Methodist, who says Jency. p. 198

8 April 1787. JOHN VICK and SYLVIA WRAY. Sur. James Bryant. Wit. Francis Young, Jr. Married by Rev. George Gurley, Rector of St. Luke's Parish, Episcopal Church. p. 51

6 March 1799. JOHN VICK and POLLEY DOUGLAS, consent of Joshua Whitney and Dolley Whitney ("for my daughter Polly Douglass"). Sur. William Spencer. Wit. Samuel Kello. (Note: Joshua Whitney m. Dolly Douglas 20 Oct. 1795). p. 126

12 March 1806. JOHN VICK and SUCKY CHITTY. Sur. Dixon Chitty.
Wit. Bolton Pierce and Samuel Kello. Married 16 March by Rev.
Exum Everett. p. 170

13 August 1781. JORDAN VICK and NANNY VICK. Sur. Simon Barrett.
Wit. Samuel Kello. p. 31

14 January 1790. JOSEPH VICK and PHEREBY DOYELL (Darrel), dau.
of Hardy Darrel. Sur. Jacob Barnes. Wit. Francis Young, Jr.
p. 64

5 May 1786. JOSHUA VICK and REBECCA HARGROVE, dau. of Augustine
Hargrove. Sur. Jacob Bailey. Wit. Richard Kello. Married 10
May by Rev. George Gurley, Rector of St. Luke's Parish, Episcopal
Church. p. 45

14 August 1789. MATTHEW VICK and ELIZABETH RAY. Sur. John
Vick. Wit. Samuel Kello and Charles Birdsong. Married 26
Aug. by Rev. George Gurley, Rector of St. Luke's Parish,
Episcopal Church. p. 61

23 February 1799. MATTHEW VICK and GLENNY WILLIAMS. Sur.
William Thomas. Wit. Samuel Kello, Jr., and William Blow.
Geney in Ministers' returns 26 Feb. Married by Rev. Benjamin
Barnes, Methodist. p. 125

5 December 1788. NOEL VICK and PATTY VAUGHAN. Married by Rev.
D.C. Barrow. Ministers' returns p. 641

15 January 1798. PARKS N. VICK and REBECCA LANKFORD. Sur.
Joseph Vick. Wit. Samuel Kello, Jr. p. 119

29 December 1777. PILGRIM VICK and LYDIA VICK. Sur. Robert
Newsum. Wit. James R. Kello. p. 25

21 June 1802. PILGRIM VICK and POLLY REVELLE or REVILL. Sur.
George Gurley, Jr. Wit. Benjamin Cobb. p. 150

3 May 1803. PILGRIM VICK and SALLY HOLT. Sur. George Genty.
Married 5 May by Rev. Benjamin Barnes, Methodist. p. 154

9 May 1754. RICHARD VICK, SR., and MARTHA WOODWARD (widow).
Sur. Joseph Gray. Wit. Richard Kello. p. 2

18 April 1786. RICHARD VICK and ELIZABETH JOHNSON of St.
Luke's Parish, now 21. Elizabeth Johnson in Ministers' returns
21 April. Joseph Vick guardian of Elizabeth. Sur. William
Johnson. Wit. Richard Kello and Maj. Samuel Kello. p. 45

8 December 1791. RICHARD VICK, Son of Arthur Vick, and ISABELL
VICK. Sur. John Pledger. Wit. John D. Haussmann. Married by
Rev. George Gurley, Rector of St. Luke's Parish, Episcopal
Church. p. 76

6 February 1778. SAMUEL VICK and ELIZABETH BARNES, both of St. Luke's Parish. Sur. William Williams. Wit. Samuel Kello. p. 25

9 January 1794. SILAS VICK and PEGGY CUTLER. Sur. William Vick. Wit. John D. Haussmann, Nancy Cutler, Rivers Reese. p. 94

8 March 1792. SIMON VICK and ESTHER ARTIS. Sur. Giles Vick. Wit. John D. Haussmann. p. 80

19 December 1794. SIMMONS VICK and ELIZABETH VICK, dau. of Arthur Vick. Sur. Jesse Woodward. Wit. Samuel Kello and Mary Vick. p. 99

10 June 1809. WILLIAM VICK and POLLY BRYANT. Sur. John Revell. Wit. Harrison Minton and Samuel Kello. Married 17 June by Rev. Benjamin Barnes, Methodist. p. 192

4 February 1782. JOHN VILVIN and CELIA HATFIELD. Ministers' returns p. 631

16 September 1783. ADAM VOFRAM and SARAH HICKS. Given as Walfram in marriage bonds. Ministers' returns p. 633

12 January 1789. NELSON WADE and PATIENCE CORBIT. Sur. Jacob Corbit. Married 15 Jan. by Rev. D.C. Barrow. p. 57

12 June 1809. RICHARD WADE and ELIZABETH FRANCIS, consent of Samuel Francis. Sur. Benjamin Turner. Wit. Samuel Kello. p. 192

11 September 1783. ADAM WALFRAM and SARAH HICKS. Sur. Benjamin Kirby. Wit. John Simmons, Jr., and Samuel Kello. See Adam Volfram. p. 37

12 December 1757. JAMES WALL and SARAH GRAY, dau. of Joseph Gray. Sur. Richard Kello. Wit. Thomas Blunt. (Consent on same paper with consent for Ann Gray). See Thomas Blunt. p. 3

1 July 1783. JAMES WALL and SALLY THOMPSON, both of Surry Co. By consent of Mr. Burges. Married by Rev. David Barrow. Ministers' returns p. 637

4 April 1801. JAMES WALL, JR. and MARY ANN MYRICK. Sur. Edmund Myrick. p. 144

20 July 1797. DREWRY WALLER and MARY JOINER. Married by Rev. Benjamin Barnes, Methodist. Ministers' returns p. 648

25 December 1801. LEVI WALLER and REBECCA JONES, dau. of David Jones. Sur. Benjamin Johnson. Wit. Samuel Kello. p. 148

15 February 1804. LEVI WALLER and MARTHA KINDRED, consent of
J. (John?) Kindred. Sur. Solomon Cooper. Wit. Benjamin Cobb,
Samuel Kello. Married by Rev. Benjamin Barnes, Methodist,
23 Feb. p. 159

10 February 1803. SAMUEL WALLICE and PEGGY HARRIS. Married
by Rev. Benjamin Barnes, Methodist. Ministers' returns p. 656

18 September 1797. JOHN LILES WARD and MARTHA FOSTER. Sur.
Arthur Foster. Wit. Samuel Kello. p. 115

18 December 1797. JAMES WARDIN (Warden) and PHEBE BALMER.
Sur. Will Edmunds. p. 118

9 February 1792. JAMES WARRELL and ACHOAH ENGLISH. Sur. Nathan
English. Wit. John D. Haussmann. p. 79

24 March 1763. BENJAMIN WARREN and RACHEL WASHINGTON of Nottoway Parish. Sur. John Warren. Wit. Edward Fisher. p. 8

29 November 1794. DRURY (Drewry) WARREN and JANE EDMUNDS,
dau. of Karenhappuch Edmunds. Sur. Edmund Wood. Wit. Richard
Kello and James Simmons. Married 23 Dec. by Rev. Robert Murrell.
p. 98

2 November 1789. JOHN WARREN, JR., and MARTHA BOOTH, dau. of
Moses Booth. Sur. Robert Rowell. Wit. Samuel Kello. p. 63

13 August 1788. MICHAEL WARREN and JEAN POWELL. Sur. James
Lundy. p. 56

5 January 1798. JAMES WASDEN (Basden) and PHEBE BALMER.
Married by Rev. Robert Murrell. Ministers' returns p. 649

7 January 1792. AMOS WASHINGTON and PAMELA BRANCH. Sur.
Goodwin Branch. Wit. John D. Haussmann. p. 77

20 February 1796. ARTHUR WASHINGTON and ELIZABETH STEWART,
widow of Benjamin Stewart. Sur. John Warren. Wit. John D.
Haussmann. p. 107

17 January 1803. ETHELDRED WASHINGTON and SARAH BRANCH, dau.
of Mary Branch. Sur. George Branch. Wit. Benjamin Cobb and
Samuel Kello. Married 20 Jan. by Rev. Drewry Lane. p. 152

6 November 1787. JAMES WASHINGTON and CELIA HANCOCK. Sur.
James Garrity. Wit. George Blunt. p. 53

14 April 1801. JOHN WASHINGTON and PATSY WILLIAMS. Sur. John
Clark. Wit. Samuel Kello. p. 144

10 March 1774. ROBERT WASHINGTON and JEAN OLIVER DAY. Sur.
Edmund Day, Jr. Wit. Richard Kello. p. 21

28 July 1803. THOMAS WASHINGTON and MARTHA JUDKINS. Married by Rev. Drewry Lane. Ministers' returns p. 653

22 January 1807. THOMAS WASHINGTON and PEGGY WINBOURNE. Sur. David W. Ritter. Wit. Samuel Kello. p. 176

18 July 1790. WILLIAM WASHINGTON and PEGGY TYLER, dau. of Edward Tyler. Sur. John Clayton. Wit. Samuel Kello. p. 66

13 October 1796. JAMES WATSON and ELIZABETH BLUNT. Sur. Chasmon Nicholson. p. 110

10 January 1793. DANIEL WEBB and POLLY GARDNER, dau. of Joshua Gardner. Sur. Josiah Vick. Wit. John D. Haussmann. p. 87

26 February 1783. BENJAMIN WELLONS and LUCRETIA CLARKE. Ministers' returns p. 632

23 December 1784. CHARLES WELLONS and SARAH CLARKE. Ministers' returns p. 635

21 August 1809. JOHN WELLONS and LUCY DREWRY. Sur. John Drewry. Wit. Harrison Minton. p. 194

14 January 1786. ROBERT WELLONS and SALLY WOOLTON (Silvier Woolon), dau. of Edward Woollon who is surety. Wit. Francis Young, Jr. p. 44

18 November 1784. WESTERN WELLONS and ANNA GARDINER. Ministers' returns p. 635

18 February 1783. WILLIAM WELLONS and ANNA VASSER. Sur. Robert Exum. Wit. Samuel Kello. Married 25 Feb. p. 36

20 December 1784. WILLIAM WELLONS and MARY POND; Polly on back of bond. Sur. Robert Exum. Wit. Samuel Kello. p. 39

16 November 1808. WILLIE (Wiley) WELLONS and RHODA PITMAN, dau. of Phebe Pitman. Sur. Samuel Pond. Wit. Benjamin Cobb. Married 17 Nov. by Rev. Drewry Lane who says Willie. p. 187

19 February 1810. ANTHONY WELLS and SALLY EDWARDS, dau. of James Edwards. Sur. Joseph Joiner. Wit. James Rochelle and Samuel Kello. p. 198

27 February 1810. GOODRICH WELLS (Wills) and REBECCA VICK. Sur. Benjamin Vick. Wit. Harrison Minton and Samuel Kello. p. 199

3 November 1800. JAMES WEST and LUCY TRAVIS (widow). Sur. William West. Married 27 Nov. by Rev. Burwell Barrett. p. 139

11 November 1793. WILLIAM WEST and CRISSEY BARROTT. Sur. Burwell Barrott. Wit. John D. Haussmann. p. 92

10 December 1795. JARRATT WESTBROOK and LUCY BLACK. Sur. Burwell Westbrook. Wit. John D. Haussmann. Lucy Blake in Ministers' returns 24 Dec. Married by Rev. Robert Murrell. p. 105

15 February 1808. JOEL WESTBROOK and REBECCA NICHOLSON. Sur. David Westbrook. Wit. John Nicholson and Benjamin Cobb. p. 183

10 August 1786. THOMAS WESTBROOK and MARGARET VASSER. Sur. Giles Joyner. Wit. Francis Young, Jr. Married 7 Sept. by Rev. George Gurley, Rector of St. Luke's Parish, Episcopal Church. p. 47

18 December 1797. DAVID WESTBROOK (Westbrook) and DARKEY (Dorcas) WESTBROOK. Sur. John J. Blake. Wit. Samuel Kello, Jr., Simon T. Westbrook and Lucy Turner. Married 27 Dec. by Rev. Robert Murrell. p. 118

2 January 1796. JOHN WESTBROOKE and BETSEY COGGIN. Sur. James Ramsey. Wit. John D. Haussmann. Married 5 Jan. by Rev. Robert Murrell who says Coggan. p. 105

6 May 1784. THOMAS WESTBROOKE and NANCY REICE. Ministers' returns p. 634

21 August 1809. THOMAS WESTBROOKE and NANCY TURNER. Sur. Samuel B. Turner. Wit. Henry Turner and Harrison Minton. p. 194

2 February 1788. GILES WESTER and SALLY EDWARDS. Sur. Francis Brag. p. 55

2 January 1783. JOHN WESTER and ANNE BURN. Ministers' returns p. 632

9 April 1789. WILLIAM WESTER (Westery) and MELCHE GARNER; Gaine on outside of bond. Sur. Frederick Parker, top of bond; Benjamin Parker at end of bond. Wit. Samuel Kello. p. 59

WESTRAY: See Wrestray

20 January 1810. GILES WESTRAY and CATHARINE DENSON. Sur. John Denson. Wit. Harrison Minton. p. 198

10 December 1804. MATTHEW WESTRAY and REBECCA GRIFFIN. Sur. Benjamin Westray. Wit. Benjamin Cobb. p. 163

23 May 1795. JOHN WHITBY of Perequimans Co., N.C., and PATTY GURLEY. Sur. George Gurley, Jr. Wit. John D. Haussmann. p. 102

12 May 1791. BENJAMIN WHITE and WINNE WILLIAMSON. Sur. William Boykin. Wit. John D. Haussmann. p. 73

8 October 1789. DAVIS WHITE and POLLY FRANCIS, dau. of Elizabeth Francis. Sur. Jesse Holt. Wit. Francis Young, Jr., and Willie Francis. This name is also given as Whitfield and Whitney. See Davis Whitfield. p. 62

14 April 1801. CAPT. JOHN WHITE of Surry Co., and SALLY ATKINSON dau. of Timothy Atkinson. Sur. Edwin Edwards. Wit. John Whitfield, Samuel Kello for George Edwards. p. 144

19 December 1798. JAMES WHITEHEAD and AGATHY WASHINGTON. Sur. William Washington. Wit. W. Evans. p. 124

20 March 1792. JOHN WHITEHEAD and KATHARINE WHITEHEAD, dau. of William Whitehead. Sur. Thomas Lane. Wit. John D. Haussmann, Nathan Bryant and Elisha E. Atkinson. p. 81

2 December 1795. LAZARUS WHITEHEAD and MARY NEWSUM. Sur. Benjamin Pinner. Wit. Samuel Kello. Married 3 Jan. 1796, by Newit Vick. p. 104

13 January 1800. RICHARD WHITEHEAD and MARGARET P. LAMB. Clarissa Whitehead mother of Margaret P. Lamb. Sur. William Evans. Wit. Samuel Kello, B.M. Johnston and Robert Downman. p. 132

5 June 1758. WILLIAM WHITEHEAD and ABBA BYNUM, dau. of William Bynum. Sur. Benjamin Bynum. Wit. Daniel Fisher, Nathan Bynum and Guy Hunley. p. 4

13 December 1781. WILLIAM WHITEHEAD and ELIZABETH BRYANT ANDREWS. Sur. Thomas Edmunds. Wit. Richard Kello. p. 31

15 January 1793. WILLIAMS WHITEHEAD and SALLY POPE, consent of Mary Pope. Sur. Benjamin Fowler. Wit. John D. Haussmann and Joseph Rollings. p. 87

9 December 1809. BENJAMIN WHITFIELD and JULIA LEARY, dau. of Edith Leary, father dead. Sur. Jonas Pope. Wit. Harrison Minton. p. 196

25 October 1789. DAVIS WHITFIELD or Whitney, and POLLY FRANCIS. Married by Rev. Robert Murrell. See Davis White. Ministers returns p. 646

25 April 1784. ELIJAH WHITFIELD and MARTHA WHITFIELD. Ministers' returns p. 634

15 January 1789. JOHN WHITFIELD and POLLY WREN of St. Luke's Parish. Sur. Stephen Handcock. Wit. Richard Kello and Samuel Kello. Married by Rev. George Gurley, Rector of St. Luke's Parish, Episcopal Church. p. 57

18 February 1792. PETER WHITFIELD and EADY HUSK. Sur. Dixon (Dickson) KILCHEN. Wit. John D. Haussmann and Josious Fargison. p. 79

23 July 1785. REUBEN WHITFIELD and PHEBE WILLSON (Phebe Whitfield on back of bond). Sur. James Maget. Wit. Francis Young, Jr. p. 41

2 August 1788. REUBEN WHITFIELD and WINNIFRED BARRETT. Sur. John Whitfield. Wit. Samuel Kello. p. 56

14 September 1801. REUBEN WHITFIELD and NANCY BEAL. Sur. Jacob Beal. Wit. Samuel Kello. p. 146

14 March 1798. SEYMOR (Seymour) WHITFIELD and PRISCILLA WHITEHEAD. Sur. Anthony Whitehead. p. 120

25 July 1782. SOLOMON WHITFIELD and SALLY HOWELL. Ministers' returns p. 631

16 December 1787. TIMOTHY WHITLEY and MARY JENKINS, both of Isle of Wight Co. Married by Rev. D.C. Barrow. Ministers' returns p. 640

21 May 1804. ELISHA WHITNEY and POLLY WHITNEY - center of bond; Elisha Joyner top and back of bond. Sur. Joshua Whitney. Wit. Benjamin Cobb. See Elisha Joyner. p. 160

18 December 1800. JOHN WHITNEY and ANNE BRACEY. Sely Bracy parent of Anne. Sur. Joshua Whitney. Wit. Samuel Kello, Jr. and Benjamin Westra. p. 140

20 October 1795. JOSHUA WHITNEY and DOLLY DUGLASS. Sur. Dempsey Douglass. Wit. Richard Kello. p. 104

5 February 1784. WILSON WIGGINS and SALLY DUNN. Ministers' returns p. 634

12 October 1795. JOSEPH WILKINS and SARAH COCKE. Sur. Francis Clements. Wit. Austin Cocke. p. 103

11 May 1786. JESSE WILKINSON and LUCY TAYLOR; Elizabeth Ridley Kello mother of Lucy. Sur. John Best. Wit. Francis Young, Jr. and John Holladay. Married 25 May by Rev. George Gurley, Rector of St. Luke's Parish, Episcopal Church. p. 46

11 February 1754. JOHN WILKINSON and ELIZABETH WILLIAMSON. Sur. Benjamin Wilkinson. Wit. Richard Kello. p. 2

20 August 1785. ABSALOM WILLIAMS and MOLLY CARR. Ministers' returns p. 636

19 January 1801. BENJAMIN WILLIAMS and MARTHA JOYNER. Sur. Jordan Joyner. Wit. Samuel Kello, Jr., and William Kitching. p. 142

27 November 1798. BRITTAIN WILLIAMS and PAMELA BELL, dau. of James Bell. Sur. William Barnes. Wit. Samuel Kello, Jr. p. 123

18 October 1791. BURRWELL WILLIAMS and ELIZABETH EDWARDS, dau. of William Edwards. Sur. Edward Williams and Drury Williams. Wit. Samuel Kello and John D. Haussmann. Married 30 Oct. by Rev. George Gurley, Rector of St. Luke's Parish, Episcopal Church. p. 75

3 January 1799. BURWELL WILLIAMS and MARTHA MOORE. Sur. John Cotton. p. 124

1 January 1789. CHARLES WILLIAMS and EDITH PARKER. Married by Rev. George Gurley, Rector of St. Luke's Parish, Episcopal Church. Ministers' returns p. 644

29 April 1784. DREWRY WILLIAMS and LEZE BEAL. Married by Rev. David Barrow. Ministers' returns p. 638

30 January 1783. EPHRAIM WILLIAMS and MARY BRYANT. Ministers' returns p. 632

5 November 1800. ETHELBERT C. WILLIAMS and LUCY WASHINGTON. Sur. Evans Williams. Wit. Samuel Kello, Jr. p. 139

22 April 1799. GEORGE WILLIAMS and NANCY HOUGH. Sur. Thomas Summerell. Wit. Samuel Kello. p. 126

28 July 1803. JAMES WILLIAMS and SALLY STEPHENSON. Sur. Charles Stephenson. Wit. Benjamin Cobb. p. 155

24 January 1810. JAMES WILLIAMS and ELIZABETH DAVIS. Sur. William Davis. Wit. John Davis. p. 198

-- March 1810. JAMES WILLIAMS and BETSEY BARRETT. Sur. John Ireland. Wit. James Rochelle. Married 11 March by Rev. Exum Everett. p. 199

25 August 1792. JEREMIAH WILLIAMS and MARY (Polly) BEAL. Sur. Drury Williams. Wit. Samuel Kello. p. 84

14 November 1798. JEREMIAH WILLIAMS and NANCY BELL. Sur. William Pebworth. Wit. William Evans and Peggy Cobb. p. 123

21 May 1810. JEREMIAH WILLIAMS and REBECCA BREWER. Sur. Drewry Williams. Wit. James Rochelle and Shadrach Cobb. p. 200

29 December 1809. JESSE WILLIAMS and ELSE WESTRAY, dau. of Giles Westray. Sur. Jonathan Westray. Wit. James Rochelle. p. 197

27 December 1788. JOHN WILLIAMS and MARY WILLIAMS. Sur. Elias Williams. Wit. Richard Kello and Milley Johnson. Married 30 Dec. by Rev. D.C. Barrow. p. 57

21 March 1792. JOHN WILLIAMS, JR., and MARTHA DAVIS. Sur. John Williams, Sr. Wit. John D. Haussmann. Married 8 April by Rev. Drewry Lane. p. 81

29 April 1803. JOHN WILLIAMS and REBECCA FOSTER. Sur. John Foster. Wit. Benjamin Cobb. p. 154

28 September 1804. KINCHEN WILLIAMS and REBECCA IVEY (Ivy), Lewis Fort guardian "for the children". Sur. Elisha Williams. Married 4 Oct. by Rev. Benjamin Barnes, Methodist. p. 162

22 December 1783. MATHEW WILLIAMS and SUSANNAH TAN (?), both of Isle of Wight Co. Married by Rev. David Barrow. Ministers' returns p. 637

12 November 1803. MATHEW WILLIAMS and MARY CLARK. Married by Rev. Drewry Lane. Ministers' returns p. 653

9 October 1809. MATTHEW WILLIAMS and SARAH FREEMAN. Sur. James Blow. Wit. Harrison Minton. p. 194

11 November 1792. RICHARD WILLIAMS and RACHAEL ATKINSON. Sur. Nathan Bryant. p. 86

26 February 1810. RICHARD WILLIAMS and WINNY WASHINGTON, dau. of James and Selah Washington. Sur. Edwin Williams. Wit. James Rochelle. p. 199

11 June 1799. SOLOMON WILLIAMS and MARCILLIA OWENS. Sur. W. Evans. Wit. Samuel Kello, Jr. Marcellia in Ministers' returns 15 June. Married by Rev. Benjamin Barnes, Methodist. p. 127

1 April 1806. SPRATLEY WILLIAMS and POLLY FARRELL BENNETT. Sur. Alexander McNiel. Wit. Benjamin Cobb. p. 170

4 July 1785. THOMAS WILLIAMS and WINNIFRED FOSTER, in bond; her signature - Winnifred Tucker, also in Ministers' returns 28 July. Sur. James Foster. p. 40

8 December 1785. WILLIAM WILLIAMS and ELIZABETH WEBB. Ministers' returns p. 636

29 January 1789. WILLIAM WILLIAMS and LYDIA JOYNER. Married by Rev. D.C. Barrow. Ministers' returns p. 641

8 February 1767. ABSALOM WILLIAMSON and RACHEL FLOWERS (Rachas Flower on back of bond), James Jones guardian of Rachel. Sur. Edward Fisher. Wit. J. Gray and John Varrell. p. 12

1 or 6 August 1761. EXUM WILLIAMSON and MILLE TURNER, dau. of Simon Turner, Sr. Sur. Daniel Fisher. Wit. J. Gray, Simon Turner, Jr., and William Turner. p. 6

6 February 1783. JOHN WILLIAMSON and MARTHA GILLIAM. Ministers' returns p. 632

12 February 1794. JOHN WILLIAMSON and REBECCA WILLIAMSON. Sur. David Williamson. Wit. John D. Haussmann. p. 95

27 October 1797. JOSEPH WILLIAMSON and SALLY CARR on face of bond, Nancy Camo on back. Sur. Edward Hatfield. Wit. Samuel Kello, Jr. p. 116

9 January 1799. JOSEPH WILLIAMSON and LUCY ROCHELLE, dau. of Judith Rochelle. Sur. Robert F. Nicholson. Wit. Samuel Kello, Jr. p. 125

8 February 1770. MATTHEW WILLIAMSON and ELIZABETH PITMAN, dau. of John Pitman. Sur. James Vaughan. Wit. Samuel Kello, James Williamson, John Carr and Will Hart. p. 15

21 January 1759. STEPHEN WILLIAMSON and ELIZABETH EDMUNDS, dau. of Howell Edmunds, Jr. Sur. John Kello. Wit. Richard Kello. p. 5

6 December 1800. TURNER WILLIAMSON of Granville Co., N.C., and BETSEY PARHAM. Sur. William Applewhite. Wit. Samuel Kello, Jr. Married 11 Dec. p. 140

19 March 1799. CHARLES WILLEFORD and PEGGY WILLEFORD. Sur. Jesse Willeford. Ministers' returns 28 Mar. p. 126

15 June 1804. JESSE WILLEFORD and FAREBE SPIVEY. Sur. Burwell Rollings. Wit. Thomas Hallcome, Fanny Hallcome. p. 160

23 April 1785. JOHNSON WILLEFORD and MOLLY JENKINS, consent of Belah Willeford. Spencer Jenkins father of Molly. Sur. Belah Willeford. Wit. Richard Kello. p. 40

11 September 1783. JESSE WILLIFORD and SUSANNA ROWE. Ministers' returns p. 633

4 March 1799. JOHN WILLIFORD (Willeford) and SARAH WILLIFORD, consent of Johnson Willeford. Sur. Jesse Williford. Wit. Samuel Kello. p. 125

28 April 1785. JOHNSON WILLIFORD and MOLLY JINKINS. Married by Rev. David Barrow. Ministers' returns p. 638

14 October 1790. THOMAS WILLIFORD and MILDRED FRANCIS, dau. of Elizabeth Francis. Sur. Jesse Holt. Wit. Willie Francis and Francis Young, Jr. Ministers' returns 21 Oct. Married by Rev. Robert Murrell. p. 67

14 February 1807. WILLIAM WILLIFORD and PATSY LONG, dau. of Lucy Long. Sur. Lion Fuller. Wit. Benjamin Cobb. p. 177

13 December 1764. FRANCIS WILLS and MIRIAM JOHNSON (Joyner on back of bond). Sur. Matthew Charles. Wit. Edward Fisher. p. 10

18 December 1809. JAMES WILLS and SALLY JOYNER, dau. of Absalom Joyner. Sur. Joseph Joyner. Wit. James Rochelle. p. 196

9 September 1790. JOHN WILLS and BETSEY BAILEY CARY. Sur. Simon Murfee. Wit. Francis Young, Jr. p. 67

13 February 1797. ROBERT WILLS and NANCY ARRINGTON, dau. of Martha Arrington. Sur. Jesse W. Moore. Wit. John D. Haussmann. Married 14 Feb. by Rev. Drewry Lane. p. 113

13 June 1771. THOMAS WILLS and ELIZABETH GRAY. Sur. John Simmons and William Urquhart. Wit. Richard Kello. p. 16

15 January 1805. THOMAS WILLS and PEGGY MURFEE. Sur. Seymour Vaughan. Wit. Samuel Kello. On same bond with Seymour Vaughan. p. 164

14 December 1786. WILLIAM WILLS and MARY CLARKE. Sur. Matthew Wills. Wit. Samuel Kello. Married 25 Dec. by Rev. George Gurley, Rector of St. Luke's Parish, Episcopal Church. p. 49

14 May 1807. JAMES WILLSON and ELIZA M. RICKS, dau. of Robert Ricks. Sur. William Randolph. Wit. William Jones. p. 179

16 August 1797. JOHN WILLSON (Wilson) and PEGGY STOREY, dau. of Samuel Storey. Sur. William Spencer. Wit. Samuel Kello. Married 18 Aug. by Rev. Benjamin Barnes, Methodist. p. 115

25 February 1796. JONATHAN WILLSON and POLLY MATTHEWS. Sur. Simon Barrett. Wit. Samuel Kello. p. 107

4 October 1810. ASA WILLSON and OLIVE BRYANT. Sur. Henry Atkins. Married by Rev. Benjamin Barnes, Methodist. p. 202

17 February 1800. BENJAMIN WILSON and PATSEY LESTER, on face of bond, Patsey Luter on back. Sur. Samuel Corbett. Wit. Jonathan Lester. Her signature "Patey Lewter". p. 134

30 December 1799. GEORGE WILSON and POLLY HUBBARD, no parents or guardian. Sur. David Spencer. Wit. Samuel Kello, Jr. Married 31 Dec. by Rev. Benjamin Barnes, Methodist. p. 131

21 March 1782. JONATHAN WILSON and MARY POPE. Ministers' returns p. 631

7 March 1786. EUSTACE WINDHAM and ELIZABETH CARR. Sur. Arthur Exum. Wit. Samuel Kello. Married by Rev. David Barrow. p. 45

29 July 1789. EUSTACE (Hustes) WINDHAM and MARTHA HUTCHINGS, consent of Mark Judkins as to Martha. Sur. Arthur Exum. Wit. Francis Young, Jr. and Mark Judkins. p. 61

3 January 1779. JOHN WINDHAM, JR. and MARTHA KITCHING, both of Nottoway Parish. Sur. Arthur Exum. Wit. Samuel Kello. p. 27

31 December 1789. WILLIAM WISTER and MELCHA GARNER. Married by Rev. George Gurley, Rector of St. Luke's Parish, Episcopal Church. Ministers' returns p. 645

12 January 1785. HOWEL WITHERS and FAITHY WOODLAND. Ministers' returns p. 635

12 January 1787. JAMES BRANTLEY WOMACK and POLLY ELLIS. Sur. Henry Turner. Married 15 Jan. by Rev. George Gurley, Rector of St. Luke's Parish, Episcopal Church. p. 50

2 April 1808. JOHN WOMACK and ELIZABETH SMITH. James B. Womack father of John. Sur. Karinto Ellis. Wit. Burk Murrell. p. 184

18 June 1810. JOSEPH J. WOMBLE and SALLY WOODWARD, dau. of John Woodward. Sur. Thomas Holleman. Wit. Jesse Womble. p. 201

20 March 1795. JOSHUA WOMBLE and MARY HART. Sur. Benjamin Bailey. Married 23 March by Rev. Drewry Lane. p. 101

25 February 1781. JAMES WOMMACK and SARAH SIMPSON. Ministers' returns p. 630

14 April 1786. BENJAMIN WOOD and CELIA GRIFFIN, consent of Thomas Griffin. Sur. Richard Kello. Wit. Francis Young, Jr. p. 45

9 June 1784. JOHN WOOD and LUCY LAWRENCE. Ministers' returns p. 634

29 July 1806. LAWRENCE WOOD and SALLY COBB, dau. of Peggy Cobb. Sur. Simon Murfee. Wit. Rice B. Pierce and Samuel Kello. p. 172

17 January 1803. THOMAS WOOD and CHERRY JONES. Sur. Jordan Jones. Wit. Benjamin Cobb. p. 152

10 June 1784. WILLIAM WOOD and LUCRETIA LAWRENCE. Ministers' returns p. 634

17 December 1795. SAMUEL WOODARD and MILLICENT JOYNER. Sur. William Evans. Married 23 Jan. 1796, by Rev. Newit Vick. p. 105

18 December 1800. SAMUEL WOODARD and CATY JOINER (Joyner), dau. of Mary Joyner. Sur. William Evans. Wit. Samuel Kello, Jr. p. 140

19 March 1796. WILLIAM WOODWARD (Woodard) and ELIZABETH BARROW, dau. of David Barrow. Sur. Nathan Barnes. Wit. Samuel Kello. p. 107

16 August 1791. WILLIAM WOOTON and SARAH GWATHNEY. Sur. Thomas Wooton. Wit. John D. Haussmann. p. 74

1 March 1790. WILLIAM WOOTON and ELIZABETH COBB. Sur. Thomas Wooton. Wit. Benjamin Drew. p. 65

19 October 1784. BENJAMIN WORRELL, JR., and MARY VICK. Ministers' returns p. 635

16 November 1807. CARY WORRELL and SALLY COUNCIL, dau. of Elizabeth Council. Sur. John Lowe. Wit. Benjamin Cobb. p. 180

24 October 1809. ELIJAH WORRELL and JULIA WORRELL. Sur. Joseph Worrell at top, Jesse Worrell at bottom. Wit. Samuel Kello. Married 26 Oct. by Rev. Benjamin Barnes, Methodist. p. 195

9 February 1792. JAMES WORRELL and ACHSAH ENGLISH. Sur. Nathan English. Wit. J.D. Haussmann. Ministers' returns p. 79

17 February 1800. JESSE WORRELL and LYDIA VICK. Sur. Holloday Revell. Wit. Samuel Kello, Jr. "Judith" Vick in Ministers' returns 27 Feb. Married by Rev. Benjamin Barnes, Methodist. p. 134

1 December 1788. JOHN WORRELL and OLIVE GRIFFIN. Sur. Thomas Bradshaw. Wit. Samuel Kello. Married by Rev. D.C. Barrow. p. 57

28 August 1779. JOSIAH WORRELL and ELIZABETH WILLIAMS, dau. of Epaphroditus Williams. Sur. Jonas Bryant. Wit. Richard Kello and Ephraim Williams. p. 28

10 September 1795. JOSIAH WORRELL and ELIZABETH WORRELL, William Newton guardian. Sur. Lewis Worrell. Wit. John D. Haussmann. p. 103

17 March 1800. JOSEPH WORRELL and RHODY WILLIAMS. Sur. Benjamin Worrell. Wit. Samuel Kello, Jr. "Rhoda" in Ministers' returns 3 April. Married by Rev. Benjamin Barnes, Methodist. p. 135

7 August 1798. LEWIS WORRELL and POLLY BAILEY. Sur. Dixon Fagurson (Forgason). Wit. W. Evans. p. 122

12 November 1795. NATHAN WORRELL and MILLEY WORRELL, dau. of Benjamin Worrell, Sr. Sur. Benjamin Worrell, Jr., who consents. Wit. John D. Haussmann. p. 104

17 December 1785. SHADRACK WORRELL and SALLY WELLONS, dau. of Charles Wellons. Sur. Charles Council. Wit. Francis Young, Jr. Married 29 Dec. by Rev. David Barrow. p. 43

5 November 1794. SHADRACK WORRELL and LYDIA COUNCIL. Sur. Charles Council. Wit. Samuel Kello. p. 98

9 August 1787. SOLOMON WORRELL and REBECCA JOHNSON, dau. of Mrs. Penninah Johnson. Sur. Absalom Joyner. Wit. Samuel Kello and Jacob Johnson. Penninah was widow of John Johnson, will proved 1783. Married 28 Aug. by Rev. David Barrow. p. 52

22 October 1800. WILLIAM WORRELL and RHODY COUNCIL. Sur.
Shadrach Worrell. p. 138

20 December 1800. WILLIAM WORRELL and SILVIA OBERRY. Sur.
William Charles. Wit. Samuel Kello, Jr. Ministers' returns
p. 140

16 December 1793. ROBERT WREN and HANNAH DAVIS. Sur. Henry
Davis. Wit. John D. Haussmann. Wren in bond - Ray in three
places. See Robert Ray. p. 92

6 April 1783. EVANS WRENN and LUCY HICKS. Ministers' returns
p. 633

15 May 1782. JOHN WRENN and POLLY LAWRENCE. Ministers' returns
p. 631

10 September 1789. RANDOLPH WRENN and MARTHA JONES. Sur.
Moses Foster. Wit. Francis Young, Jr., and Henry Myrick.
Married 12 Sept. by Rev. George Gurley, Rector of St. Luke's
Parish, Episcopal Church. p. 62

16 January 1804. BENJAMIN WRESTRAY and NANCY LOW. Sur. Nathan
Westray. Wit. Jesse Bracy. p. 158

18 March 1784. JAMES WRIGHT and LUCY CARROLL. Married by
Rev. David Barrow. Ministers' returns p. 638

16 February 1786. JAMES WRIGHT in bond, William Wright in 3
places and in Ministers' returns 2 March, and ANN DREW, dau.
of Mrs. Nancy Drew. Consent of Col. William Blunt as to groom.
Sur. John Wright. Wit. Francis Young, Jr., and William Blunt.
p. 44

2 March 1786. WILLIAM WRIGHT and ANN DREW. Ministers' returns
p. 636   See James Wright.

7 July 1807. WILLIAM WYNNE and CHARLOTTE FORT. Sur. Benjamin
Lewis. Wit. Samuel Kello. p. 179

21 October 1784. THOMAS WYNNS (Wynne) and SUSANNA MANEY.
Ministers' returns p. 635

15 February 1796. WILLIAM YOUNG and CHARLOTTE REVILL. Sur.
Edward Hatfield. Wit. John D. Haussmann. p. 106

Blythe,		
Abigail	62	
Charlotte	105	
Bools, Lydia	70,107	
Boon,		
Alsea	44	
Eady	43	
Booth-Boothe,		
Elizabeth	2,64	
Holland	4	
Lucy	13	
Martha	111	
Rebecca	2	
Sally	57	
Selpah	54	
Bosman, Sally	25	
Boush, Margaret	99	
Bouth, Margaret	99	
Bowden-Bowdain,		
Elizabeth	8	
Milly	20	
Bowen, Eliza	63	
Bowers,		
Jeasey	21	
Sally	20	
Sarah	61	
Boyd, Elizabeth	56,83	
Boykin,		
Avey	18	
Eliza	104	
Elizabeth	36	
Louisa	14	
Mary Ann	18	
Nancy	93	
Patsy	19	
Patsy Moss	83	
Polly	34	
Sarah	(2) 95	
Bracer, Frances	46	
Bracy,		
Anne	115	
Cherry	33	
Patience	61	
Bradshaw,		
Angelina	51	
Elizabeth	104	
Honour	67	
Lydia	90	
Mary	87	
Mason	87	
Polly	38	
Tabitha	36	
Branch,		
Diana	34	
Hannah	61	
Lucy	41	
Pamela	111	
Sarah	111	
Brantley,		
Lucy	38	
Mary	38	
Nancy	54	
Brasey, Miriam	40	
Brewer,		
Holland	10	

Brewer, cont'd.		
Martha	28,83	
Rebecca	116	
Brickett, Judith	92	
Bridgers, Milley	66	
Bridges, Nancy	18	
Briggs,		
Ann	49	
Betsey	5	
Emely	85	
Frances	28	
Martha	40	
Nancy	74	
Sally	81	
Brister-Bristow,		
Frances	(2) 30	
Hannah	38	
Lucy	99	
Mary	27	
Penelope	31	
Polly Howard	46	
Ruth	101	
Britt,		
Anne	29	
Betsey	18,50	
Caty	57	
Cherry	65	
Elizabeth	79	
Janet	100	
Levenia	7	
Lydia	20	
Mary	1	
Milly	98	
Molly	32	
Nancy	20	
Patsey	18	
Polly	62	
Rebecca	106	
Rhoda	48	
Sarah	72,101	
Sally	17	
Thamer	100	
Brittle, Elizabeth	15	
Brown-Browne,		
Elizabeth	84	
Esther	54	
Fanny	59	
Lucretia	84	
Parthenia	84	
Browning,		
Lucy	79	
Polly	51	
Bryant,		
Alsey	5,90	
Ann	14	
Elizabeth	22	
Lycia	49	
Mary	85,116	
Olive	119	
Patsy	26	
Pheraba	38	
Polly	110	
Sally	8,22,23,26	
Tempy	85	
Bunn, Millicent	18	
Burgess,		
Elizabeth M.	68	
Sally	3	
Burn, Anne	113	

Busby, Sally	56	
Butler,		
Jemima	46	
Lilley	63	
Butts,		
Betsy	15	
Lucy	2	
Nancy	58	
Pally	27	
Polly	81	
Sarah	96	
Buxton, Grizzet	26	
Bynum,		
Abba	114	
Frances	74	
Polly	8	
Byrd,		
Ann	12	
Tabitha	94	
C		
Calvert,		
Fanny	63	
Mary	85	
Polly	64	
Calthorpe,		
Anna	100	
Dinah	69	
Eleanor Clifton	86	
Sarah	106	
Cambell, Charlotte	100	
Camo, Nancy	118	
Camp, Mary	76	
Capell, Polly	12	
Carr,		
Abigail	71	
Eady	9	
Elizabeth	119	
Honour	25	
Mary Jane	73	
Molly	93;115	
Mourning	45	
Nancy	68	
Priscilla	10	
Rodia (Rhodesia)	45	
Sally	22,118	
Carrell,		
Jane	21	
Sarah	(2) 25	
Carroll,		
Lucy	122	
Polly	21	
Cary-Carey,		
Betsey Bailey	119	
Peggy	99	
Unity	99	
Cathon, Mary	50	
Caton, Pherebe	3	
Chalmers, Sally	16	
Champion, Mary	70	

Pitman, cont'd.
Priscilla 50
Rhoda 112
Sarah 16,40

Pledger, Nancy 99

Pond,
Mary 86,112
Nancy 78
Patsey 86
Sally 34
Sarah 34
Temperance A. 96

Pope,
Ann 88,108
Charity 31
Charlotte 79
Christian 45
Elizabeth 11,106
Fanny 9,15,42
Mary 119
Mourning 57
Nancy 60,94,97
Patience 57,67
Patsy 94
Phebe 24
Polly 49,88
Prudence 46
Rachel 5
Sally 28,87,88,114

Porter,
Delilah 91
Mary 65
Milly 31
Polly 33
Rebecca 18
Sarah 10
Tabitha 89
Temperance 85

Powell-Powel-Powall,
Betty 105
Blytha 3
Jean 111
Mason 3
Nancy 36
Parthenia 6
Patsey 20
Rebecca 20
Sa-ly 46
Sophia 89
Temperance 37

Powers, Martha 66

Pursell, Mary 31

Reece, cont'd.
Polly 43,59
Rebecca 9
Sally 59
Suckey 59
Sukey 66
Sylvia 78

Revelle-Revill,
Charlotte 122
Mourning 61
Polly 109

Ricks,
Eliza M. 119
Teresa 102

Riddick,
Mildred 75
Patty 75
Priscilla 85

Ridley,
Jane 1,83
Mary 14
Pamela 57
Peggy 21
Rebecca 74
Sarah 38

Rivers,
Charlotte 44
Edith 81

Rives, Elizabeth 103

Roberts, Mary 73

Rochelle, Lucy 118

Roe, Jerusha 10

Rogers,
Mary H. 103
Polly 103

Rollins-Rollings,
Phoebe 99
Sally 63

Rosser, Nancy 49

Rowe,
Lucy 78
Susanna 118

Ruffin,
Lucy 59
Sarah 102

Scott,
Amey 91
Mary 13
Sarah 4
Susanna 19

Seay, Judith Baker 83

Sebrell, Averilla 64

Seward, Sarah 103

Seyburn, Delilah 64

Shield,
Elizabeth 101
Nancy 99

Simpson, Sarah 120

Simmons,
Ann 68,83
Elizabeth 103
Frances 39
Lucy 11,29,95
Mary 26,63,79,86,107
Mary Cocke 79
Milly 66
Nancy 94
Patience 92,103
Rebecca 95
Sylvia 66

Slade, Mary 50

Smith,
Elizabeth 5,120
Hannah 101
Lucy 9,94
Polly-Polley 31,105
Rebecca 91

Speed,
Betsey 97
Elizabeth 100
Mille 62
Pamelia 3
Sarah 62

Speight, Susanna 15

Spencer,
Edith 88
Elizabeth 44

Spivy-Spivey,
Dinah-Diana 46
Ferebe 118
Peggy 82

Stamp, Ann 11

Starks, Polly 41

Staunton, Lucy 13

Stephens, Polly 22

Stephenson, Mary 55

Steward-Stewart,
Ann M. 81
Elizabeth 111
Mary 58
Mason 58
Nancy 43
Rebecca 103
Sally 56
Suky 42

Stokes, Rebecca 30

Storey-Story,
Amey 58

www.ingramcontent.com/pod-product-compliance
Lightning Source LLC
Chambersburg PA
CBHW021832020426

42334CB00014B/594